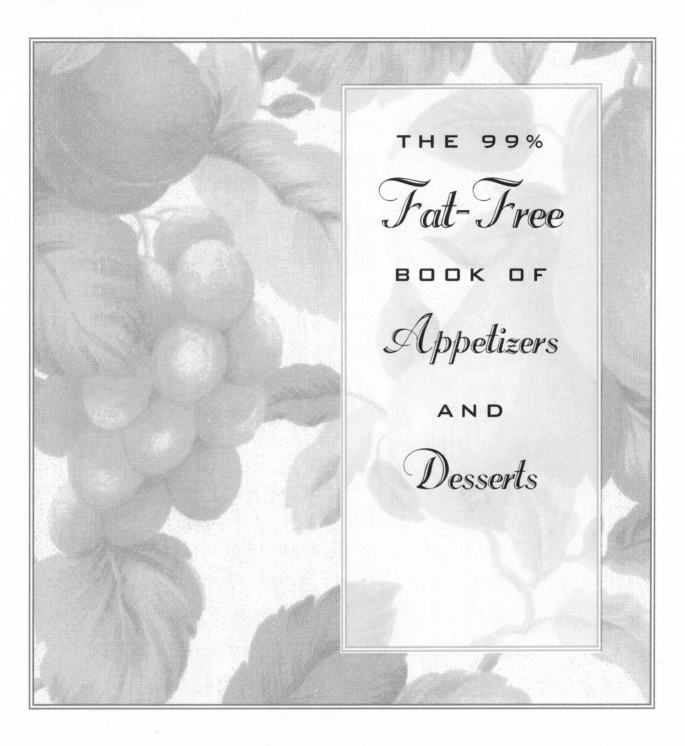

THE 99%
Fat-Free
BOOK OF
Appetizers
AND
Desserts

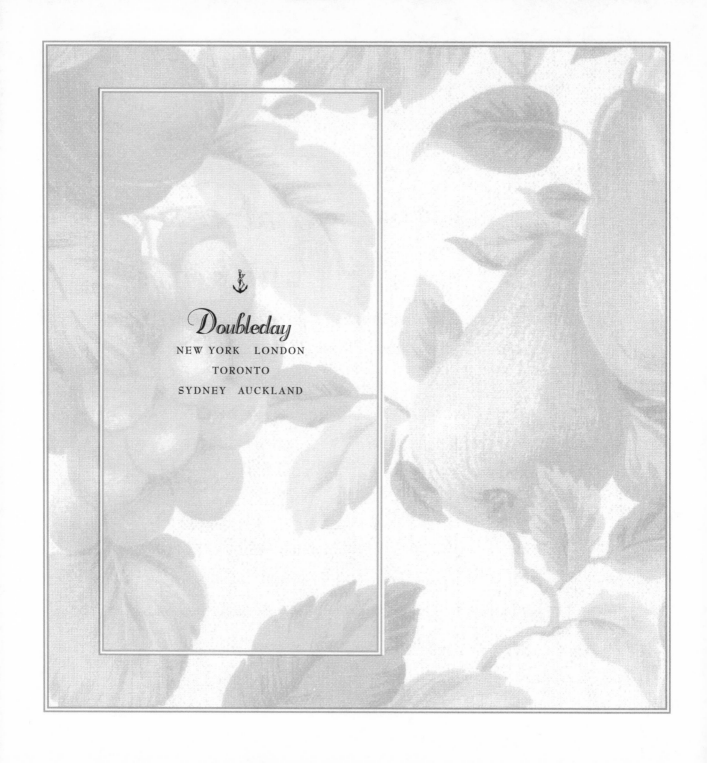

Doubleday

NEW YORK   LONDON

TORONTO

SYDNEY   AUCKLAND

THE 99%

Fat-Free

BOOK OF APPETIZERS

AND DESSERTS

STYLISH AND SATISFYING
WAYS TO START AND FINISH
YOUR MEAL WITH LESS THAN
1 GRAM OF FAT

Barry Bluestein
AND *Kevin Morrissey*

PUBLISHED BY DOUBLEDAY
a division of Bantam Doubleday Dell Publishing Group, Inc.
1540 Broadway, New York, New York 10036

DOUBLEDAY and the portrayal of an anchor with a dolphin
are trademarks of Doubleday,
a division of Bantam Doubleday Dell Publishing Group, Inc.

Book design by Marysarah Quinn

Library of Congress Cataloging-in-Publication Data
Bluestein, Barry.
The 99% fat-free book of appetizers and desserts : stylish and satisfying ways to start
and finish your meal with less than 1 gram of fat / Barry Bluestein & Kevin Morrissey.
— 1st ed.
p.   cm.
Includes index.
1. Low-fat diet—Recipes. 2. Appetizers. 3. Desserts. I. Morrissey, Kevin.   II. Title.
III. Title: Ninety-nine percent fat-free book of appetizers and desserts.
RM237.7.B58 1995
641.5'638—dc20   95-1042
                                                                                         CIP

ISBN 0-385-47924-7

10   9   8   7   6   5   4   3   2   1

FIRST EDITION

Acknowledgments

We gratefully acknowledge the assistance of Ann Bloomstrand, who was often there to offer a helping hand or a creative twist.

For invaluable advice and commentary as this book took shape, we thank Eleanor Bluestein, Colin Reeves, William Rice, and Jill Van Cleave; for recipe ideas, Martha Scheuneman and Merrilyn Siciak. We owe so many for their ongoing support of our work—Philip Ansalone, Elaine Barlas, Cheryl Blumenthal, Meredith Brunswick, Sally and Arnold Cohen, Rosie Daley, Lisa and Lou Ekus, and Claudia Clark Potter.

We thank our editor, Judith Kern, for her belief in our vision, her steady guiding hand, and her wry wit. A tip of the toque to all the folks at Doubleday, including Paola Fernandez Rana, Valerie Peterson, and Brandon Saltz, for doing what they do so well.

Contents

Introduction

In recent years, Americans have awakened to the dangers of foods high in fat and embarked enthusiastically on a quest for a healthier table. The wide-ranging interest in low-fat cooking is evident everywhere—from cookbook shelves to carryout counters, from restaurant menus to frozen-food cases.

In *The 99% Fat-Free Cookbook*, we introduced a revolutionary and comprehensive approach to low-fat cooking, distinguished by its diner-friendly perspective. By showing the cook how to eliminate virtually all fat at the source, in the kitchen, it frees diners from regimented diets and allows healthful eating without deprivation.

The 99% Fat-Free Book of Appetizers and Desserts utilizes the same philosophy and techniques to help today's health-conscious cooks tackle the two most challenging aspects of menu planning—appetizers (including hors d'oeuvres and plated first courses) and desserts.

Selection of a main course is the simplest step in planning a meal, a decision often driven by what looks good at the market or what's on hand in the freezer. First and last courses require more forethought and planning. Festive and indulgent by definition, appetizers and desserts pose perhaps the greatest challenge to the aspiring low-fat cook.

In *The 99% Fat-Free Book of Appetizers and Desserts*, we offer more

than 125 recipes for eminently stylish and satisfying appetizers and desserts with less than one gram of fat per portion.

Fat-free cooking entails the discriminating selection and innovative preparation of ingredients, not the banishment of favorite dishes from our menus. We have broken traditional recipes and methodologies down to their basic components and rebuilt them in ways that eliminate superfluous fats, which contribute little to intrinsic flavor.

It's not necessary to eliminate meat, poultry, seafood, and other wonderful fresh components from our repertoire of favorite appetizers—just to use them judiciously to enhance flavor rather than as main ingredients.

Nor is it necessary to banish chocolate dishes from the fat-free kitchen, just to prepare them with cocoa powder mixtures instead of ingredients derived from cocoa butter.

Delectable desserts of all sorts can be made utilizing combinations of rich buttermilk, evaporated skim milk, and nonfat yogurt and ricotta cheese to replace fatty dairy products; using egg whites, nonfat egg substitutes, fruit purees, and corn syrup to replace egg yolks and shortenings; and often with fruit juice concentrates in lieu of sugar.

We offer an array of recipes for healthy dishes, ranging from comfort foods to the cutting edge, from updated classics to increasingly popular international selections, from the excruciatingly easy to dishes that require just a bit more effort, and from recipes that yield enough for an intimate dinner party to those that can easily fill a buffet.

Through *The 99% Fat-Free Book of Appetizers and Desserts,* we strive to enable healthy cooks to banish fully the fatty and the bland from their menus, from start to finish!

Total fat per portion has been calculated for each recipe to the nearest $1/100$th of a gram, and total calories to the nearest $1/10$th of a calorie.

For commercial ingredients, we use the lowest-fat brands readily available. Always read and compare product labels carefully.

To give you a better idea how much produce to buy at the market, equivalents are provided for ingredient measures, unless the measured quantity is derived from less than a whole fruit or vegetable, along with the desired weight of whole ingredients. For example:

1 cup chopped white onion
   (about 1 onion);

$1/2$ tablespoon chopped garlic
   (about 2 cloves);

2 large red bell peppers
   (14 to 16 ounces).

BEANS: A few of our recipes call for the use of canned beans when the added convenience won't compromise taste. As there are commercial brands available that have less fat than beans cooked at home, the actual amount of fat per portion may be a bit higher for these recipes if you use dried beans.

BISCUITS: We use flaky, low-fat Buttermilk Biscuits (page 10) in some of our dessert recipes. They're also great to keep on hand for making little sandwiches—just the right size for a quick appetizer or snack.

BREAD: Several commercial brands now offer a selection of light breads, some of which are relatively low in fat; compare nutritional labels. Our French Bread (page 9) is significantly lower in fat than most commercial products we have found. In recipes that specifically call for French Bread in the ingredients list, the fat count is based upon our bread's use.

BREAD CRUMBS: As all of the prepared bread crumbs we know of have a higher fat content than we budget for this ingredient, we make our own. One slice of bread yields 4 to 5 tablespoons of bread crumbs. Use French Bread (page 9) or one of the low-fat commercial products.

CHICKEN STOCK: We strongly recommend that you make your own Chicken Stock (page 6), which provides greater control over taste and fat content. It will keep for up to three days in the refrigerator and can be frozen in handy 2-cup portions in airtight plastic bags. If you use commercial chicken stock, refrigerate and then skim and strain before heating, according to our recipe directions.

COCOA POWDER: Recipes are based upon use of Dutch processed cocoa powder, which produces a different chemical reaction than other cocoas that are not treated with an alkali. Compare product labels among Dutch or European-style cocoa powders, which vary in fat content.

CORN: Although frozen corn generally contains less fat than fresh, our recipes, unless otherwise specified, have been written and fat counts calculated to allow for the use of fresh.

EGG SUBSTITUTE AND EGG WHITE: We use both egg white and liquid egg substitute (the variety that can be stored in the freezer and kept far longer than shell eggs). In most of our recipes, they can be used interchangeably; the exceptions are those recipes that call for both and the Potato and Pepper Frittata (page 65), which needs the color provided by the egg substitute.

Read egg substitute labels thoroughly; be sure to choose a *nonfat* product and avoid those that contain oil or tofu.

GROUND MEAT: Don't use packaged preground meat, which contains a considerable amount of fat (even preground turkey). Have your butcher trim and grind the lean cuts called for in our recipes or prepare it yourself using a food processor, a meat grinder, or the grinder attachment to a stationary electric mixer.

HERBS AND SPICES: We use fresh herbs, now readily available in many supermarkets, in volume. Although the fresh variety is preferable for most recipes in which an herb is a principal seasoning, dried herbs can be substituted in a pinch. Use only about a third as much of the dried as you would of the fresh.

There's no substitute, however, for freshly ground black pepper; keep a pepper mill handy. As freshly grated nutmeg can add a real flavor boost to many dishes, we try to keep a little nutmeg and a fine grater in the pantry.

JUICE: Freshly squeezed lemon and lime juice really do make a difference, and require virtually no extra effort beyond remembering to keep a supply on hand. If you substitute commercial orange juice for freshly squeezed, use a variety that is not made from concentrate.

MILK: We call for skim milk, buttermilk, and evaporated skim milk in our recipes. Buttermilk, contrary to the popular misconception, is made from skim milk and contains little or no butterfat. Compare nutrition labels for evaporated skim milks, which can vary in fat content even between different products from the same manufacturer.

PASTA: We prefer our own fresh Pasta (page 8), which is much lower in fat than most commercial products, unless preparing a dish that requires a more complicated shape of noodle.

RICE: Several brands of rice are well within our guidelines for fat content if cooked without butter.

ROASTED PEPPERS: A few recipes, in which the added step will make a difference, call for roasting bell peppers from scratch. In other cases, you can use commercially prepared roasted peppers.

To roast bell peppers, preheat the broiler and line the rack with aluminum foil. Cut the pepper in half lengthwise, core, and seed. Place on the rack, cut side down, 2 to 3 inches from the heat source. Broil for about 5 minutes, until charred. Carefully transfer to an airtight plastic bag and let cool for about 10 minutes, after which the skin should rub off easily.

SALT: We use coarse kosher salt in all but baking recipes. Readily available in most supermarkets, kosher salt has less sodium per measure than finer grain table salt.

SUN-DRIED TOMATOES: Sun-dried tomatoes can be purchased prepared or dried at home. To dry your own tomatoes, preheat the oven to 140 degrees. Cut plum tomatoes in half lengthwise and place them on a cookie sheet, cut side up. Bake for about 18 hours, until the tomatoes are dry, a deep reddish brown in color, and still somewhat elastic. Do not allow them to blacken or become brittle.

TOMATOES: A few recipes call for the use of canned tomatoes, when the added convenience won't compromise taste. (Canned tomatoes are actually preferable to hothouse tomatoes, since the canned varieties are allowed to ripen longer on the vine.) In all other cases, the amount of fat per portion has been calculated to allow for the use of fresh tomatoes, which contain more fat than many canned products.

TORTILLAS: The fat content of corn tortillas varies widely. Read nutritional labels carefully.

VEGETABLE STOCK: It's best to make your own easy Vegetable Stock (page 7); the few commercial products we've seen tend to include ingredients that add fat to the stock. Ours has a refrigerator shelf life of five days and can be frozen in 2-cup portions in airtight plastic bags for future use.

WON TON WRAPPERS: We recently discovered how useful won ton wrappers, sometimes called dumpling skins, can be in low-fat cooking. Readily available in Asian groceries and some supermarkets, they are virtually fat-free and come preformed, thus eliminating the time and effort involved in making the dough for many hors d'oeuvres from scratch. Baked and sprinkled with sugar, they can be used as pastry shells for desserts.

YOGURT CHEESE: To make yogurt cheese, suspend a yogurt funnel (available from kitchenware stores) or a strainer that has been lined with a coffee filter atop a nonreactive bowl. Empty plain or vanilla nonfat yogurt into the funnel or strainer and place the bowl in the refrigerator for at least 8 hours (preferably overnight) until all the liquid whey has dripped through into the bowl. The substance remaining in the funnel or strainer is pure yogurt cheese.

Chicken Stock

4 pounds chicken bones, with a few
scraps of meat left on

3 carrots, trimmed and cut into chunks
(unpeeled)

2 parsnips, trimmed and quartered
lengthwise (unpeeled)

1 large yellow onion, peeled and cut
into 1-inch chunks

5 stalks celery, trimmed and quartered

15 sprigs fresh parsley, ends trimmed

Water to cover 2 inches above
ingredients (about 20 cups)

12 whole black peppercorns

Put the chicken bones, vegetables, and parsley in a large stockpot. Cover
with water. Bring to a rapid boil over high heat, then skim the foamy
residue off the top. Reduce the heat to low and simmer for about 4 hours,
uncovered, until the bones begin to disintegrate. Periodically skim the
residue off the top.

Remove the pot from the heat. Discard all solid ingredients from the
stock and strain the liquid into a large bowl. Add the peppercorns. Refrigerate, uncovered, for at least 2 to 3 hours. If refrigerating overnight,
cover after 2 to 3 hours.

When you take the stock out of the refrigerator, use a large spoon to
lift off as much of the layer of fat that has settled on top as possible. Using a dinner knife, scrape along the top of the stock to catch any additional small pieces of fat. Place the stock in a large pot and cook over
medium heat for 2 to 3 minutes, until it has turned from a gelatinous
state back into liquid. Pour the liquefied stock through a strainer lined
with a double layer of cheesecloth (to strain sediment) into a clean bowl.

YIELD—ABOUT 1²/₃ QUARTS

Vegetable Stock

1 large yellow onion, coarsely chopped

2 medium leeks, trimmed, rinsed, and sliced

2 tomatoes (or 6 plum tomatoes), coarsely chopped

4 carrots, peeled and coarsely chopped

4 cloves garlic

3 stalks celery, trimmed and sliced

10 sprigs fresh parsley, ends trimmed

6 whole black peppercorns

4 bay leaves

4 quarts water

Combine all the ingredients in a large stockpot. Bring to a boil over medium-high heat. Reduce the heat to low and simmer gently, uncovered, for 2 hours. Strain into a large bowl, pressing down on the vegetables to extract as much liquid as possible.

YIELD—ABOUT $1^{2}/_{3}$ QUARTS

Pasta

2 cups all-purpose flour   ¾ cup nonfat liquid egg substitute

Put the flour into the bowl of a food processor. Pulse while adding the egg substitute. This will produce a soft ball of dough.

Turn the dough out onto a floured board and knead it into a single ball that is glossy and elastic. Enclose in plastic wrap and set aside for 30 minutes.

Flour the rollers of a pasta machine. Cut the dough in quarters, flour all over, and flatten. Put the first piece through the largest opening on the pasta machine 3 times, folding the dough in half after each time through. Then put the dough through each successively smaller opening, until it has gone through the smallest. Repeat this process for the remaining 3 pieces of dough.

Put each of the thin pieces of dough through the wide cutters on the pasta machine. Hang and dry the strands of pasta for about 10 minutes.

YIELD—1 POUND

French Bread

¹/₄ cup lukewarm water (105 to 115 degrees on an instant-read thermometer)

¹/₂ teaspoon sugar

1 packet quick-rise yeast

3 cups bread flour

¹/₂ teaspoon salt

³/₄ cup plus 2 tablespoons skim milk, at room temperature

¹/₂ teaspoon cornmeal

1 large egg, white only, mixed with 1 tablespoon water

5 ice cubes

Put the water and sugar into a small bowl. Sprinkle the yeast on top and set aside for a few minutes, until the mixture is bubbly.

Combine the bread flour and salt in the bowl of a food processor and process for 1 minute. Scrape in the yeast mixture. Turn the machine back on and drizzle the skim milk through the feed tube until a dough ball forms, then process for 45 seconds to 1 minute more.

Put the ball in a bowl, cover with a moist towel, and place in a warm (around 80 degrees) spot for about 1¹/₂ hours, until the dough has doubled in size.

Punch the dough down, fold it in, and transfer it to a work surface that has been dusted with flour. Flatten the dough, shape it into a rectangle, and roll it up into a 15-inch loaf.

Place the loaf on a nonstick cookie sheet that has been dusted with the cornmeal. Recover with the moist towel and set aside for about 1 hour more, until the dough no longer springs back to the touch.

Preheat the oven to 425 degrees.

Paint the loaf with the egg white and water wash and make 4 diagonal slashes in the top. Put 3 of the ice cubes directly onto the bottom of the oven and bake the bread on the cookie sheet for 5 minutes.

Add the remaining ice and bake about 25 minutes more, until the bread is brown and sounds hollow when tapped. Cool on a wire rack.

YIELD—1 LOAF OR ABOUT THIRTY ¹/₂-INCH SLICES

Buttermilk Biscuits

2¹/₂ cups all-purpose flour

1 tablespoon baking powder

1 teaspoon baking soda

¹/₄ teaspoon salt

3 tablespoons nonfat cream cheese

2 tablespoons nonfat sour cream

1 cup buttermilk

Light vegetable oil cooking spray

2 tablespoons skim milk

Preheat the oven to 400 degrees.

In a large mixing bowl, stir together the flour, baking powder, baking soda, and salt. Using a pastry blender or 2 dinner knives, cut in the cream cheese and sour cream. Stir in the buttermilk.

With lightly floured hands, gather the dough into a ball, knead in the crumbs, and transfer to a floured surface. Roll out to a thickness of ¹/₂ inch. With a glass or a cookie cutter, cut out eight 2¹/₂-inch circles.

Spray a nonstick baking sheet once lightly with the vegetable oil spray and spread the oil over the surface. Put the dough circles on the sheet and brush them with the skim milk. Bake for about 12 minutes, until lightly browned. Remove the baking sheet from the oven and let the biscuits cool.

YIELD—8 BISCUITS

Appetizers

Meat

AND

Poultry

Minted Turkey Meatballs

1 pound turkey breast tenderloin, trimmed

3 slices light oatmeal bread, crust removed, torn into chunks

¹/₄ cup water

1 large egg, white only

¹/₂ cup finely grated yellow onion

1 teaspoon chopped garlic (1–2 cloves)

¹/₂ cup finely chopped fresh mint

1 teaspoon ground cumin

1 teaspoon dried oregano

¹/₈ teaspoon freshly ground black pepper

Salt to taste

Light vegetable oil cooking spray

Preheat the oven to 425 degrees.

Process the turkey in a food processor until finely chopped. Add the bread and water and process until a doughlike ball forms. Remove to a large mixing bowl and add the egg white, onion, garlic, mint, cumin, oregano, pepper, and salt. Work by hand until all ingredients are well combined. With moistened hands, form into 24 meatballs, using 2 tablespoons of the mixture for each.

Spray a nonstick baking sheet once lightly with the vegetable oil spray and spread the oil evenly over the surface. Place the meatballs on the sheet. Bake for 3 minutes, turn, and bake for about 3 minutes more, until crispy brown.

YIELD—24 MEATBALLS

Fat per meatball—0.27 g.

Calories per meatball—27.1

This popular Greek meze, or appetizer, is traditionally prepared with lamb. For our lighter and healthier version, we've replaced the lamb with turkey. The meatballs are quite good on their own, and also go especially well with Cucumber Mint Dip (page 89).

Somewhat Eurasian in derivation, this delicacy employs a seasoned nonfat ricotta mixture, evocative of rich and creamy Boursin, to add flavor and texture to the classic Italian beef role. It's sliced into bite-size medallions that can be served hot or cold. Served cold, the braciola pairs well with a soy-vinegar dipping sauce of Asian origin.

If baby asparagus is unavailable, quarter larger asparagus spears lengthwise.

Asparagus and Ricotta-Stuffed Braciola

8 ounces baby asparagus spears, trimmed

1/4 cup nonfat ricotta cheese

1 tablespoon buttermilk

2 teaspoons finely chopped shallot

1/2 teaspoon minced garlic

1/4 teaspoon dried thyme

One 8-ounce top round steak, at least 1/2 inch thick, trimmed

Salt and freshly ground black pepper to taste

DIPPING SAUCE
(OPTIONAL):

1/4 cup reduced-sodium soy sauce

2 tablespoons cider vinegar

1/2 teaspoon snipped fresh chives

Preheat the oven to 375 degrees.

Bring a saucepan of water to a boil. Add the asparagus and blanch for about 3 minutes, until the spears turn bright green. Immediately remove to a colander and rinse well with cold running water. (The asparagus may also be blanched in a microwave oven. Cover and microwave at full power for about 1 minute.)

Combine the ricotta cheese, buttermilk, shallot, garlic, and thyme in a bowl. Mix thoroughly and set aside.

With a sharp knife, slice the steak horizontally into 2 pieces, each about 1/4 inch thick. Place each piece between 2 sheets of wax paper and pound with a meat tenderizer, rolling pin, or rubber mallet to a thickness of about 1/8 inch.

Spread half of the ricotta mixture onto one of the pieces of steak. Lay half of the asparagus spears on top lengthwise, trimming the ends if necessary to allow a 1/4-inch border of meat at each end. Sprinkle with salt and pepper. Starting with a long end, roll up and secure in 3 places with string. Repeat the process for the second piece of steak.

Transfer the braciola to a baking dish lined with aluminum foil and bake for about 30 minutes, until crusty brown.

Remove from the oven and cool for 10 minutes. Cut off the string and slice each roll into ¹/₂-inch medallions.

Serve warm or cold with dipping sauce.

YIELD—24 MEDALLIONS AND ABOUT
6 TABLESPOONS DIPPING SAUCE

Fat per medallion—0.37 g.; per tablespoon of dipping sauce—0.02 g.

Calories per medallion—19.5; per tablespoon of dipping sauce—5.4

Veal Satay

Redolent of ginger, this light rendition of a favorite Indonesian snack is flavorful enough to stand on its own, making the fat-laden peanut dipping sauce that accompanies the traditional version unnecessary.

2 tablespoons reduced-sodium soy sauce

1 tablespoon rice vinegar

1/2 tablespoon honey

1 teaspoon minced garlic (1–2 cloves)

1 tablespoon finely grated fresh ginger

1 teaspoon ground cumin

1/2 teaspoon ground coriander

4 ounces veal scaloppine (from top round leg), trimmed and cut into eight 4- × 1-inch strips

Soak eight 8-inch bamboo skewers in water for at least 1 hour.

Combine the soy sauce, vinegar, honey, garlic, ginger, cumin, and coriander in a mixing bowl. Add the meat, mix well, cover, and marinate at room temperature for 1 hour.

Preheat the broiler.

Thread each of the marinated veal strips onto a skewer. Wrap the exposed ends of the skewers with aluminum foil (remove before serving). Broil as close to the heat source as possible for 1 minute, turn, and broil for 1 minute more.

YIELD—8 SKEWERS

Fat per skewer—0.34 g.
Calories per skewer—23.5

Steamed Pork and Chicken Dumplings

4 ounces boneless pork tenderloin, trimmed and cut into chunks

4 ounces boneless, skinless chicken breast, cut into chunks

¼ cup sliced water chestnuts, finely chopped

1½ teaspoons reduced-sodium soy sauce

1 tablespoon dry sherry

1 scallion, white part only, finely chopped

¼ cup chopped fresh spinach

1 large egg, white only

48 square won ton wrappers

3 cups water

Finely chop the pork and chicken chunks in a food processor, or work the meat through a grinder fitted with the disc with the smallest holes.

Combine the ground meat with the water chestnuts, soy sauce, sherry, scallion, spinach, and egg white. Mix thoroughly.

Spoon about a teaspoon of the mixture into the center of a won ton wrapper. Dab a little water around the outer border. Gather the corners of the wrapper together and pinch closed to form a pouch. Repeat the process until all the dumplings are stuffed.

Bring the water to a boil in a wok over high heat and reduce the heat to medium. Fit the wok with a rack. Stand the dumplings in a single layer on a heat-resistant plate and set the plate on the rack. Cover and steam for 4 minutes.

Serve immediately.

YIELD—48 DUMPLINGS

Fat per dumpling—0.19 g.

Calories per dumpling—29.8

Substituting chicken for half the pork called for in traditional recipes brings these scrumptious little dumplings well within the healthy range. We've also added water chestnuts for a bit of crunch.

This recipe can easily be cut in half; but as the dumplings freeze well, we suggest making the larger quantity even if you're planning an intimate dinner party. For a quick and healthy won ton soup, just add them to Chicken Stock (page 6).

Chicken Tamales

Many health-minded cooks are unduly intimidated by the thought of attempting Mexican dishes, which are perceived as inherently high in fat.

These tasty tamales derive their thick, rich texture from buttermilk rather than pork fat. Besides, they're great fun—served up authentically in corn husks (found in Mexican groceries and in the ethnic section of many supermarkets) that diners themselves peel before eating the tamales. We like to serve the tamales with Corn Salsa (page 86).

2 large dried ancho chile peppers	1 1/2 teaspoons salt
1 cup boiling water plus boiling water to cover corn husks	8 ounces skinless, boneless chicken breast, trimmed and cut into cubes
12 dried corn husks	1 cup instant yellow cornmeal
1/2 teaspoon chopped garlic	1 teaspoon baking powder
1/2 teaspoon dried oregano	3/4 cup Chicken Stock (page 6)
1/4 teaspoon ground coriander	3 tablespoons buttermilk
1/4 teaspoon sugar	

Combine the dried chile peppers and 1 cup of the boiling water in a small bowl. In another bowl, cover the dried corn husks with boiling water. Set both aside for about 30 minutes, until soft.

Remove the chile peppers, reserving the soaking liquid. Stem the peppers and break them open. Core, seed, and devein. Transfer to the bowl of a food processor. Strain 1/2 cup of the soaking liquid into the processor. Add the garlic, oregano, coriander, sugar, and 1/2 teaspoon of the salt. Process until a smooth sauce is formed. Remove to a saucepan, stir in the chicken, cover, and cook over medium-low heat for 20 minutes.

Meanwhile, mix the cornmeal, baking powder, and the remaining teaspoon of salt in a small bowl. Put the chicken stock into a small saucepan and warm it over medium heat just until it gives off steam. Remove from the heat and whisk in the cornmeal mixture. Whisk in the buttermilk, one tablespoon at a time, continuing to whisk until the texture turns from crumbly to thick and smooth.

Remove a corn husk from the soaking liquid, pat dry, and place it on a work surface with the tip pointing away from you. Put a heaping tablespoon of the cornmeal mixture onto the husk and spread it to cover an area about 5 inches wide and 3 inches long, leaving at least a 1-inch border at the top and bottom. Mound a scant tablespoon of the chicken mixture in the center. Fold one, then the other side of the husk in, overlapping the sides by about ¹/₂ inch. Fold the top down and the bottom up. Place the husk seam side down into a steamer basket.

Continue the process until all corn husks are done. Steam the tamales for about 40 minutes over boiling water, until firm.

YIELD—12 TAMALES

Fat per tamale—0.57 g.
Calories per tamale—78.7

Mediterranean Stuffed Tomatoes with Veal

8 medium tomatoes
   (about 2½ pounds)

1 cup chopped white onion
   (about 1 onion)

2 tablespoons water

6 ounces ground veal scaloppine
   (from top round leg)

1 cup cooked white rice

¼ cup seedless raisins

⅓ cup chopped fresh flat-leaf parsley

1½ teaspoons ground cinnamon

½ teaspoon ground allspice

¼ teaspoon salt

⅛ teaspoon freshly ground
   black pepper

¼ cup dry white wine

Preheat the oven to 350 degrees.

Slice ¼ to ½ inch off the top of each tomato, reserving the tops. Scoop out and discard the pulp and seeds from inside the tomato. Place the tomatoes in a 9-inch round pie plate, tightly packed to keep them upright.

In a large nonstick frying pan, cook the onion and water for about 5 minutes over medium heat, until the onion is translucent. Add the veal and continue to cook until the veal is no longer pink, about 2 minutes, stirring and breaking up the meat as it cooks.

Remove the pan from the heat and add the cooked rice, raisins, parsley, and dry seasonings. Stir until well combined.

Stuff each tomato with a generous ⅓ cup of the mixture. Put the tops back on loosely. Pour the wine into the pie plate, around the tomatoes.

Bake for about 30 minutes, until the tomatoes are fork tender.

Plate and serve.

YIELD—8 SERVINGS

Fat per serving—0.92 g.
Calories per serving—113.5

Turkey Sausage en Croûte

1 pound turkey breast tenderloin, trimmed and cut into chunks

$^1\!/_2$ tablespoon aniseseed

2 teaspoons dried thyme

$^1\!/_2$ teaspoon dried oregano

$^1\!/_2$ teaspoon paprika

$^3\!/_4$ teaspoon salt

$^1\!/_8$ teaspoon freshly ground black pepper

$^1\!/_8$ teaspoon red pepper flakes

2 cloves garlic, peeled

1 recipe French Bread (page 9), prepared through the first rise

2 tablespoons Dijon-style mustard

1 teaspoon cornmeal

1 large egg, white only, mixed with 1 tablespoon water

$^3\!/_4$ teaspoon all-purpose flour

Preheat the oven to 375 degrees.

Put the turkey into a mixing bowl. Add the aniseseed, thyme, oregano, paprika, salt, and peppers. Mix well to coat the turkey. Transfer to a food processor and add the garlic. Process to a fine chop. (You should have about $1^1\!/_2$ cups of sausage meat.)

Put the sausage in a nonstick frying pan. Cook for about 7 minutes over medium heat, stirring occasionally, until the meat is no longer pink.

Punch the French bread dough down and divide it in half. On a lightly floured work surface, roll out each half to about 12 × 6 inches. Coat each with 1 tablespoon of the mustard and top with about $^3\!/_4$ cup of the sausage mixture. Roll up lengthwise and crimp the edges closed.

Dust a nonstick baking sheet with the cornmeal. Put the stuffed loaves onto the pan, seam side down, and paint with the egg white and water wash. Dust with the flour.

Bake for 30 to 35 minutes, until hollow when tapped. Remove from the oven and let the loaves sit for 10 minutes before cutting each one into twenty-four $^1\!/_2$-inch slices.

YIELD—48 SLICES

Fat per slice—0.24 g.
Calories per slice—38.6

Based on a classic pâté baked in a pastry crust, this exceptionally healthy rendition is a bonus on any buffet. It's flavorful, filling, easy to make, and it holds up well.

The sausage en croûte also freezes well, so we recommend making a full recipe and freezing one loaf when cooking for a smaller gathering.

These filling morsels are best piping hot. Serve immediately, or on a hot plate for a buffet. Apple Chutney (page 92) makes a zesty accompaniment.

Savory Meat-Filled Pastries

1 cup all-purpose flour

$^1/_2$ teaspoon salt

5 tablespoons buttermilk

$^1/_4$ cup plain nonfat yogurt

4 ounces veal scaloppine (from top round leg), trimmed

2 ounces top round steak, trimmed

$^3/_4$ cup chopped white onion

1 tablespoon seeded and finely chopped jalapeño pepper

$^1/_2$ teaspoon freshly grated ginger

Light vegetable oil cooking spray

Preheat the oven to 425 degrees.

Combine the flour and salt in a mixing bowl. Add the buttermilk and yogurt and mix with a wooden spoon. Finish mixing by hand, working the dough until smooth and forming it into a ball. Cover and set aside.

Grind the veal and beef in a food processor. Transfer to a nonstick frying pan. Add the onion, jalapeño pepper, and ginger. Cover and cook over low heat for 15 minutes, stirring occasionally. Remove the pan from the heat and allow the meat to cool.

Turn the dough onto a lightly floured work surface and roll out to about 9 × 12 inches, squaring the corners by hand. With a sharp knife, cut the dough into twelve 3-inch squares.

Mound $2^1/_2$ teaspoons of the filling in the center of each square. Moisten the outer edges a bit with water. With lightly floured fingers, fold each square up into a triangle and crimp securely closed.

Spray a nonstick baking sheet once lightly with the vegetable oil spray and spread the oil evenly over the surface. Put the pastries on the sheet and bake for 10 minutes.

Remove the baking sheet from the oven, spray the pastries twice with the vegetable oil spray, turn them over, and bake for 5 to 10 minutes more, until golden brown all over.

YIELD—12 PASTRIES

Fat per pastry—0.70 g.

Calories per pastry—59.2

Turkey and Leek Rolls

1 cup freshly squeezed orange juice

$^2/_3$ cup white wine vinegar

2 teaspoons finely grated fresh ginger

$^1/_2$ tablespoon dried oregano

$^1/_4$ teaspoon salt

$^1/_4$ teaspoon freshly ground
black pepper

1 tablespoon plus 1 teaspoon minced
garlic (about 5 cloves)

Eight 2$^1/_2$-ounce turkey breast cutlets

9–10 ounces leek, trimmed to white
and light green parts, cut in half
lengthwise, rinsed, and thinly sliced
crosswise (about 1 cup)

$^1/_3$ cup freshly squeezed lime juice

2 teaspoons white wine Worcestershire
sauce

In a large mixing bowl, combine the orange juice, vinegar, ginger, oregano, salt, black pepper, and 1 tablespoon of the garlic. Add the turkey, mix to coat, cover, and set aside to marinate at room temperature for 1 hour.

Mix the remaining 1 teaspoon of garlic, the leek, lime juice, and Worcestershire sauce in a second bowl. Set aside while the turkey is marinating.

Preheat the oven to 350 degrees.

Remove the turkey cutlets from the marinade. Put 2 tablespoons of the leek mixture in the center of each cutlet. Roll up, secure with toothpicks, and place the rolls in a baking pan lined with aluminum foil. Cover with another sheet of aluminum foil and bake for 20 minutes.

Remove the baking pan from the oven and turn on the broiler. Remove the foil cover and broil the turkey and leek rolls for a minute or two, just to lightly brown.

YIELD—8 SERVINGS

Fat per serving—0.88 g.

Calories per serving—102.8

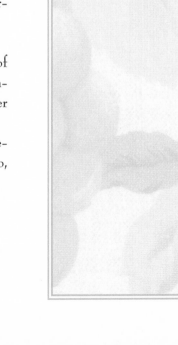

Generous portions of turkey, steeped in a refreshing orange marinade, are paired here with the ever-popular leek. They make a simple and elegant first course.

Chicken Yakitori

2 tablespoons reduced-sodium
    soy sauce

1 tablespoon dry sherry

1 tablespoon rice vinegar

1 tablespoon dark brown sugar,
    firmly packed

$^1\!/_2$ tablespoon minced garlic
    (about 2 cloves)

1 tablespoon finely grated fresh ginger

8 ounces skinless, boneless chicken
    breast, trimmed and cut into 16
    cubes (about $1^1\!/_4$-inch cubes)

3 ounces green bell pepper, cut into
    sixteen 1-inch cubes

2 scallions, trimmed to white and light
    green parts, quartered crosswise

Combine the soy sauce, sherry, vinegar, brown sugar, garlic, and ginger in a mixing bowl. Add the chicken, mix thoroughly, cover, and marinate at room temperature for 1 hour.

Meanwhile, soak eight 8-inch skewers in water.

Preheat the broiler.

On each skewer, intersperse 2 chunks of chicken, 2 bell pepper cubes, and a piece of scallion. Wrap the exposed ends of the skewers with aluminum foil. Position as close as possible to the heat source and broil for 2 minutes; turn, and broil for another 2 minutes.

YIELD—8 SKEWERS

Fat per skewer—0.45 g.

Calories per skewer—45.5

Curried Chicken in Endive Boats

8 ounces skinless, boneless chicken breast, trimmed

2/3 cup plain nonfat yogurt

1 1/2 cups peeled and diced Granny Smith apple (about one 8-ounce apple)

3/4 cup chopped fresh pineapple

1/2 cup finely diced celery (1–2 stalks)

2 teaspoons curry powder

1/2 teaspoon salt

1/4 teaspoon freshly ground black pepper

12 leaves Belgian endive

Steam the chicken over boiling water for about 20 minutes, until fork tender. Let cool for a few minutes, cut into chunks, and set aside.

Put the yogurt into a mixing bowl. Add the apple, pineapple, celery, curry powder, salt, and pepper. Add the chicken and mix thoroughly. Cover and chill.

Top each endive leaf with about 1/4 cup of chilled chicken salad and serve.

YIELD—12 ENDIVE BOATS

Fat per boat—0.43 g.
Calories per boat—42.0

This recipe derives its distinctive character from a generous boost of curry powder, which tickles the palate even as it soothes the spirit with its heady aroma. Actually, this is a range of recipes, since the taste will vary greatly depending upon the type and strength of curry powder used.

Encased in leaves of Belgian endive, the curried chicken is equally at home on a plate or a buffet.

Shredded Pork and Bok Choy Goyza with Ginger Dipping Sauce

8 ounces baby bok choy cabbage, leaves separated

6 ounces boneless pork tenderloin, trimmed and very thinly sliced

1 large scallion, trimmed and finely chopped

2 teaspoons dry sherry

1 tablespoon reduced-sodium soy sauce

1 teaspoon hoisin sauce (optional)

14 round won ton wrappers

Light vegetable oil cooking spray

DIPPING SAUCE:

3 1/2 tablespoons reduced-sodium soy sauce

1 tablespoon rice vinegar

1/2 tablespoon finely grated fresh ginger

1/4 teaspoon minced garlic

1 teaspoon thinly sliced scallion rounds, white and light green parts only

1/2 teaspoon sugar

1/8 teaspoon freshly ground black pepper

Steam the cabbage for about 6 minutes over boiling water, until fork tender. Finely chop. Squeeze excess water from the chopped cabbage and transfer the cabbage to a mixing bowl. Add the pork and scallion and mix well. Mix in the sherry and soy sauce and, if desired, the hoisin sauce. Cover and refrigerate for at least 5 minutes.

For the dipping sauce, combine all ingredients and mix well. Set aside.

Mound a tablespoon of the chilled pork and cabbage mixture in the center of each won ton wrapper and dab water around the outer edge of the circle. Fold in half and secure closed with overlapping pleats.

Place in a deep-sided nonstick frying pan and add enough water to cover the bottom third of the goyza. Bring to a boil over high heat, cover, and boil for 3 minutes. Remove from the heat and let the goyza cool in the pan for 2 to 3 minutes.

Transfer the goyza to a plate. Discard the water from the frying pan and wipe it clean and dry. Preheat over a high heat until beads of water flicked into the pan sizzle. Spray the pan twice with the vegetable oil spray. Reduce the heat to medium, return the goyza to the pan, and cook until the bottoms are dark brown and crusty, about 3 minutes. The goyza (also known as pot stickers) will stick to the pan at first; they're done when they move easily if you shake the pan.

Serve with the dipping sauce.

Yield—14 goyza

Fat per goyza (including dipping sauce)—0.87 g.
Calories per goyza (including dipping sauce)—47.3

We prefer these hearty South American turnovers baked in delicate, flaky phyllo. In addition to reducing fat and calories, this method of preparation puts the spotlight on the savory blend of beef and seasonings inside, where it belongs. All too often, empanadas are fried in a heavy dough, which can overpower the filling.

Beef and Baked Potato Empanadas

¹/₄ cup seedless raisins

2 tablespoons golden rum

4 ounces top round steak, trimmed and cut into chunks

1 cup chopped yellow onion (about 1 onion)

¹/₂ teaspoon chopped garlic

¹/₄ cup boiling water

1 teaspoon ground cumin

1 teaspoon paprika

¹/₄ teaspoon dried oregano

¹/₂ teaspoon salt

Pinch of cayenne pepper

4 ounces baked potato (about half an Idaho potato that has been baked, peeled, and broken up)

6 sheets phyllo dough

About ³/₄ cup Chicken Stock (page 6)

Combine the raisins and rum in a small bowl and set aside to soak.

Put the meat in the bowl of a food processor and pulse until finely chopped. Transfer to a nonstick frying pan and add the onion and garlic. Cook over medium heat for about 10 minutes, stirring frequently, until lightly browned. Add the boiling water and seasonings. Reduce the heat to medium-low and cook for about 5 minutes more, until the mixture is fairly dry and aromatic.

Remove the meat mixture to a bowl. Mix in the baked potato with a fork. Add the raisins and rum. Cover and refrigerate for at least 15 minutes. (The recipe can easily be prepared up to this step the day before serving.)

Preheat the oven to 375 degrees.

Place six 18- × 12-inch sheets of phyllo dough on a work surface and cover them with a damp towel to keep them from drying out.

Remove the first sheet and paint it lightly with chicken stock. Lay a second sheet directly on top. Cut into six 3- × 12-inch pieces. Put a rounded tablespoon of the meat and potato filling in the bottom right-hand corner of each piece. Grasp the corner and fold the dough up over the filling to form a triangule. Continue to fold the dough up as you would a flag, making 5 more triangular folds, then fold the small flap at the top under.

Repeat the process until all 18 empanadas are filled and formed. Place the empanadas flap side down on a large baking sheet that has been lined with baker's parchment, and paint each with chicken stock.

Bake for 20 to 25 minutes, until golden brown.

YIELD—18 EMPANADAS

Fat per empanada—0.43 g.
Calories per empanada—53.6

This dish is as colorful as it is flavorful. The dark green pepper sits on a base of vibrant red coulis, which is also drizzled on top. The filling is a medley of hearty lentils and delicate wild rice, with a welcome accent of beef.

Peppers Stuffed with Steak and Wild Rice on Tomato Coulis

Eight 5-ounce green bell peppers

$^1/_3$ cup wild rice

$^1/_3$ cup dried lentils

$2^1/_2$ cups water

1 beef bouillon cube

5 ounces top round steak, trimmed and
    cut into cubes

1 small white onion (about 6 ounces),
    cut into chunks

$^1/_3$ cup chopped scallions
    (about 3 scallions)

$^3/_4$ teaspoon Worcestershire sauce

$^1/_4$ teaspoon salt

$^1/_8$ teaspoon freshly ground
    black pepper

One 16-ounce can crushed tomatoes

$^1/_4$ teaspoon dried oregano

Slice $^1/_4$ to $^1/_2$ inch off the top of each pepper and discard. Scoop the core and seeds from the pepper, running a knife around the inside cavity to remove residual veins. Set aside.

Combine the rice and lentils in a colander. Rinse well and pick over. Bring the water to a boil in a small saucepan. Stir in the rice, lentils, and bouillon cube. Bring back to a boil, cover, reduce the heat, and simmer for 30 minutes. Remove the pan from the heat.

Put the beef and onion chunks in a food processor and pulse to a fine chop. Transfer to a large nonstick frying pan. Cook over medium heat for about 10 minutes, stirring occasionally, until lightly browned. Remove from the heat and stir in the scallion, Worcestershire sauce, salt, pepper, and the wild rice and lentil mixture.

Pour the crushed tomatoes into a Dutch oven. Add the oregano. Stuff each bell pepper with $^1/_2$ cup of the filling and stand upright in the Dutch oven, spooning a little tomato over the peppers. Bring to a boil over medium heat, cover, reduce the heat, and simmer for 30 to 35 minutes, until the peppers are fork tender.

Serve the peppers on the tomato coulis with a little drizzled over the top as well.

YIELD—8 SERVINGS

Fat per serving (including coulis)—0.95 g.
Calories per serving (including coulis)—131.4

Smoked Turkey Tacos with Salsa

Eight 6-inch corn tortillas

SALSA:

1 cup seeded and roughly chopped tomato (about 1 tomato)

1/2 cup fresh corn kernels

1/4 cup chopped red onion

1 tablespoon seeded and finely chopped jalapeño pepper

1 tablespoon chopped fresh cilantro

1 tablespoon freshly squeezed lime juice

FILLING:

8 ounces smoked turkey breast meat, shredded

1 teaspoon minced garlic (1–2 cloves)

2 tablespoons water

1 tablespoon chopped fresh cilantro

1 cup chopped green-leaf lettuce

Preheat the oven to its lowest setting.

Wrap the tortillas in a slightly damp towel and place them in the oven, along with the plates on which the tacos will be served.

For the salsa, combine the tomato, corn, onion, jalapeño pepper, and cilantro in a mixing bowl. Add the lime juice and toss to mix thoroughly.

In a nonstick frying pan, heat the turkey, garlic, water, and cilantro for about 2 minutes over medium heat, stirring constantly.

On each warm plate, place a tortilla. Scatter 2 tablespoons of the lettuce on the tortilla and top with 2 1/2 tablespoons of the filling. Roll up and top with 1/4 cup of the salsa.

Serve immediately.

YIELD—8 SERVINGS

Fat per serving (including salsa)—0.78 g.

Calories per serving (including salsa)—70.0

Seafood

Shrimp Toast

4 ounces peeled and deveined shrimp

2 scallions, white and light green parts only, cut into chunks

$^{1}/_{2}$ cup sliced water chestnuts

1 teaspoon dry sherry

1 teaspoon reduced-sodium soy sauce

1 large egg, white only

Pinch of white pepper

9 slices light white bread

Preheat the broiler.

Combine the shrimp, scallions, water chestnuts, sherry, soy sauce, egg white, and pepper in a food processor. Process to a smooth paste (about $^{3}/_{4}$ cup).

Place the bread on a large baking sheet lined with aluminum foil. Toast the bread on one side in the broiler and remove. Turn the bread over, spread a scant teaspoon of the shrimp paste on each slice, making sure to cover it completely, and quarter on the diagonal to make 4 triangles.

Return the baking sheet to the broiler and broil for 2 minutes. Rotate the baking sheet 180 degrees and broil for about 1 minute more, until the tops are toasted.

YIELD—36 TRIANGLES

Fat per triangle—0.14 g.
Calories per triangle—15.8

Quick, extremely low in fat and calories, and all too often overlooked by the home cook.

Halibut, Wild Mushrooms, and Baby Vegetables in Parchment Packets Drizzled with Warm Buttermilk Sauce

1 ounce mixed dried wild mushrooms

1 1/2 cups boiling water

One 8-ounce halibut steak

16 baby asparagus spears

4 baby carrots, peeled and cut into
  julienne strips

1/2 teaspoon minced garlic

1 tablespoon finely chopped shallot

1/2 teaspoon dried thyme

3 tablespoons water

1/4 cup dry white wine

Salt and freshly ground black pepper
  to taste

BUTTERMILK SAUCE:

1 cup reserved mushroom soaking
  liquid

1 tablespoon white wine vinegar

1 tablespoon arrowroot

1/2 cup buttermilk

Combine the dried mushrooms and boiling water in a small bowl. Cover and set aside to soak for at least 25 minutes.

Cut two 16- × 24-inch pieces of baker's parchment into four 8- × 12-inch rectangles each.

Slice the halibut horizontally to form 2 equal pieces half the thickness of the original steak. Cut each piece into quarters.

Trim the asparagus to the length of the halibut fillets. Bring a large saucepan half filled with water to a boil. Add the asparagus and boil for 1 minute. Add the carrots and boil for 2 minutes more. Drain and rinse under cold running water for 15 seconds.

Drain the mushrooms, reserving the soaking liquid. Squeeze out as much water as possible, coarsely chop, and transfer to a small nonstick frying pan. Add the garlic, shallot, thyme, and the 3 tablespoons of water. Sauté over medium-low heat for about 2 minutes, stirring occasionally, until the mixture is dry. Add the wine and cook for an additional 5 minutes.

Preheat the oven to 400 degrees.

Fold each of the parchment rectangles in half crosswise, crease the parchment to form a seam, and open. Put a piece of halibut into the center of each packet along the seam. Mound a tablespoon of mushrooms on each. Season with salt and pepper. Top each with 2 asparagus spears and a scattering of carrots.

To seal the packets, grasp the ends of the parchment parallel to the inner seam and fold down about $1/4$ inch. Fold in the sides and fold the corners over to secure closed.

Place the packets on a large baking sheet and bake for 10 minutes. Remove from the oven when done.

While the packets are baking, strain 1 cup of the reserved mushroom soaking liquid into a small saucepan. Add the vinegar. Bring to a boil over medium-high heat and boil for 8 to 10 minutes, until the liquid is reduced to $1/4$ cup.

Remove the pan from the heat and let sit for 2 minutes. Dissolve the arrowroot into the buttermilk and slowly whisk the mixture into the saucepan. Return to low heat and whisk constantly just until the sauce begins to give off steam, about 1 minute.

Transfer each halibut packet to a serving plate, slit open the parchment, and drizzle about a tablespoon of the sauce over the fish and vegetables.

YIELD—8 SERVINGS

Fat per serving (including sauce)—0.77 g.
Calories per serving (including sauce)—62.6

Fish Wellington in Mushroom Pâté

1 pound white button
   mushrooms, cleaned
   and chopped

1/4 teaspoon dried thyme

3/4 teaspoon salt

3/8 teaspoon freshly ground
   black pepper

1 cup evaporated skim milk

4 sheets phyllo dough

1 large egg, white only, mixed with
   2 tablespoons water

12 ounces monkfish, outer membrane
   removed

Cook the mushrooms in a nonstick frying pan over medium-high heat, stirring constantly, just until they're lightly browned and beginning to give off liquid, about 2 minutes.

Stir in the thyme, 1/4 teaspoon of the salt, 1/8 teaspoon of the pepper, and the evaporated skim milk. Reduce the heat and simmer, uncovered, for at least 15 minutes, until the mixture has thickened.

Transfer the contents of the pan to the bowl of a food processor or blender and puree. Cover and refrigerate for 1 hour.

Preheat the oven to 350 degrees.

Lay a sheet of phyllo dough out on a work surface. Paint with the egg white and water wash. Lay 3 more sheets on top, painting between the layers. Spoon the mushroom pâté along the length of the dough, leaving a 1/4-inch margin, and spread it inward onto the surface of the dough.

Place the monkfish on top of the pâté along the outer edge. Sprinkle the remaining 1/2 teaspoon of salt and 1/4 teaspoon of pepper on top.

Lift the edge of the dough along the filling and roll it up into a long log, encasing the fish in the pâté and layers of dough.

Gently transfer the log to a baking sheet that has been lined with baker's parchment, placing the log seam side down, and paint the exposed surface with the wash. Bake for about 45 minutes, until golden brown.

Remove the fish Wellington to a platter and let it sit for 5 minutes before slicing.

YIELD—12 SLICES

Fat per slice—0.73 g.
Calories per slice—71.3

Escargots in Mushroom Caps

12 large white button mushrooms
  (about $3/4$ pound)

$1/3$ cup chopped shallots
  (about 2 shallots)

1 tablespoon chopped garlic
  (3–4 cloves)

2 tablespoons water

$1/2$ cup dry white wine

12 giant French helix snails
  (about one 7-ounce can)

$1/4$ cup homemade bread crumbs
  (see Pantry)

Preheat the oven to 350 degrees.

Clean and stem the mushrooms. Place them into a baking dish in a single layer, cap side down.

Combine the shallots, garlic, and water in a nonstick frying pan. Warm over medium-low heat until the shallots are translucent and the water has evaporated, about 2 minutes. Add the wine and snails. Raise the heat to medium and cook for about 3 minutes more, until the wine is reduced by half.

Stuff a snail into each mushroom cap. Spoon about a teaspoon of the shallot and garlic mixture from the frying pan over each snail, topping with a teaspoon of the bread crumbs.

Bake for 15 minutes. Turn on the broiler and broil the stuffed mushrooms just until dark brown and crusty, about 1 minute.

YIELD—12 STUFFED MUSHROOMS

Fat per mushroom—0.20 g.
Calories per mushroom—44.7

New Potatoes Filled with Caviar Cream

2 tablespoons nonfat ricotta cheese

1 1/2 tablespoons plain nonfat yogurt

1/4 teaspoon freshly squeezed
     lemon juice

3/4 teaspoon chopped fresh dill

1 teaspoon diced red onion

1/2 ounce (1 tablespoon) red lumpfish
     caviar

12 small new red potatoes
     (1–1 1/4 pounds)

Put the ricotta into a mixing bowl. Add the yogurt and blend until smooth. Mix in the lemon juice, dill, and onion. Add the caviar. Cover and chill.

Cook the potatoes in a microwave oven at full power for 2 to 3 minutes, until fork tender. (They can also be baked in a 350 degree oven for about 20 minutes.)

Cut the potatoes in half and place them on a serving dish, cut side down. Using a melon baller or a sharp knife, make a well in the top of each, scooping out about 3/4 teaspoon.

Mound some of the caviar cream into each well and serve.

YIELD—24 POTATOES

Fat per potato—0.23 g.

Calories per potato—17.1

This is a quick and economical recipe for a sure crowd pleaser. It can be prepared in a few minutes and actually works best with the hearty, supermarket variety lumpfish caviar.

Coquilles St. Jacques

³/₄ cup dry white wine

³/₄ cup Chicken Stock (page 6)

6 whole black peppercorns

1 small stalk celery, with leaves, broken in half

1 bay leaf

1 sprig fresh flat-leaf parsley

1 shallot, peeled and thinly sliced

8 ounces white button mushrooms, cleaned, stemmed, and sliced

2 tablespoons water

8 ounces bay scallops

2 tablespoons buttermilk

2 tablespoons all-purpose flour

6 tablespoons skim milk

¹/₄ cup evaporated skim milk

2 tablespoons nonfat liquid egg substitute

¹/₂ teaspoon salt

Pinch of cayenne pepper

1 tablespoon freshly squeezed lemon juice

Light vegetable oil cooking spray

¹/₂ tablespoon freshly grated Parmesan cheese

³/₈ teaspoon paprika

Bring the wine and chicken stock to a boil in a saucepan over high heat. Add the peppercorns, celery, bay leaf, parsley, and shallot. Reduce the heat to low and simmer, uncovered, for 10 minutes.

Meanwhile, combine the mushrooms and the water in a large frying pan. Cook over medium heat for about 10 minutes, stirring occasionally, until the mushrooms are limp and dry. Transfer to a large bowl.

Rinse out the frying pan and strain in the wine and chicken stock. Bring back to a boil. Reduce the heat to low, add the scallops, cover, and poach for 5 minutes. With a slotted spoon, transfer the scallops to the bowl with the mushrooms. Turn the heat up to high and boil the poaching liquid until it is reduced by half, about 4 minutes.

For the sauce, combine the buttermilk and flour in a small saucepan, whisking thoroughly until blended. Add 2 tablespoons of the poaching liquid and whisk until smooth. Over medium-low heat, slowly whisk in the rest of the poaching liquid and then the skim milk. Continue to whisk for 1 minute more. Remove the pan from the heat.

Preheat the oven to 400 degrees.

Combine the evaporated skim milk and the liquid egg substitute in a small bowl. While whisking, add ¼ cup of the sauce mixture from the small saucepan, then whisk the combination back into the saucepan. Bring to a simmer over medium heat, whisking constantly, about 2 minutes. If the sauce is thick enough to coat the back of a spoon, remove it from the heat; if not, continue to cook and whisk a bit longer. Whisk in the salt, cayenne pepper, and lemon juice.

Pour the sauce over the mushrooms and scallops and mix well.

Spray six 4-ounce gratin dishes or ramekins, or six scallop shells, lightly with the vegetable oil spray and place them on a baking sheet. If using shells, line the sheet with aluminum foil. Put ⅓ cup of the mixture in each, top with ¼ teaspoon of the Parmesan cheese, and dust with paprika.

Bake for about 15 minutes, until bubbly. Turn on the broiler and broil for 30 seconds to brown.

YIELD—6 SERVINGS

Fat per serving—0.99 g.

Calories per serving—97.6

This tasty first course works equally well as an hors d'oeuvre if chilled and sliced into rings after baking. Prepare the tomato sauce separately while the squid chills, and serve it on the side.

Spanish Stuffed Squid

8 large cleaned squid (about 12 ounces)

One 28-ounce can Italian plum tomatoes, drained, seeded, and coarsely chopped

1/2 teaspoon sugar

1 cup dry white wine

1 cup finely chopped white onion (about 1 onion)

2 teaspoons minced garlic (2–3 cloves)

2 tablespoons finely chopped fresh flat-leaf parsley

1/8 teaspoon freshly grated nutmeg

1/4 teaspoon salt

1/8 teaspoon freshly ground black pepper

3 tablespoons water

1 cup homemade bread crumbs (see Pantry)

2 tablespoons dry sherry

Preheat the oven to 350 degrees.

Remove and finely chop the fins and tentacles of the squid.

Combine the tomatoes, sugar, and white wine in a small saucepan over medium-low heat. Cook for about 10 minutes, until slightly thickened.

Meanwhile, put the chopped fins and tentacles into a nonstick frying pan. Add the onion, garlic, parsley, nutmeg, salt, pepper, and water. Cook over medium heat for about 5 minutes, stirring occasionally, until the onions are soft and translucent. Add the bread crumbs and sherry. Stirring constantly, continue to cook just until the sherry is absorbed, about 30 seconds.

Stuff about 2 tablespoons of the mixture from the frying pan into each squid and secure closed with a toothpick.

Spread half the tomato sauce on the bottom of a baking dish large enough to hold the squid in a single layer. Arrange the squid on top of the tomato sauce and cover with the remaining sauce. Cover the pan tightly with aluminum foil. Bake for 20 minutes.

Transfer the squid to individual plates, remove toothpicks, and spoon some tomato sauce over each.

YIELD—8 SERVINGS

Fat per serving (including sauce)—0.76 g.
Calories per serving (including sauce)—103.8

For these flavorful hors d'oeuvres, we prefer the firmer, flakier texture of dried salt cod to that of fresh. It takes a while to reconstitute the dried cod, but the procedure is simple. Put the dried cod up to soak around dinnertime a day in advance, changing the soaking water before going to bed and again first thing the next morning.

The Salt Cod Balls go nicely with our cool and refreshing Cucumber Mint Dip (page 89).

8 ounces dried salt cod

1 cup finely chopped yellow onion (about 1 onion)

$^1/_2$ teaspoon minced garlic

2 tablespoons water

$1^1/_2$ tablespoons tequila

1 cup all-purpose flour

$^3/_4$ teaspoon baking powder

$^1/_8$ teaspoon salt

$^1/_8$ teaspoon cayenne pepper

1 large egg, white only

$^1/_2$ cup buttermilk

1 tablespoon nonfat sour cream

1 tablespoon seeded and finely chopped red jalapeño pepper

2 tablespoons finely chopped fresh cilantro

Light vegetable oil cooking spray

$^1/_2$ teaspoon paprika

1 cup homemade bread crumbs (see Pantry)

Break the cod into large pieces. Place it in a mixing bowl and cover with cold water. Set aside to soak for at least 12 hours, at room temperature, until reconstituted into fluffy pieces of fish, changing the water twice in the interim.

Rinse in a colander under cold running water, drain, and transfer to a large saucepan. Add sufficient cold water to cover the fish by 1 inch. Bring to a boil over high heat and boil for 1 minute. Drain, refill with water to cover by an inch, and bring back to a boil. Reduce the heat to low and simmer for about 20 minutes, uncovered, until the fish flakes easily.

Drain, remove any residual skin or bone from the fish, and flake.

Combine the onion, garlic, and the 2 tablespoons of water in a medium nonstick frying pan. Cook over medium-low heat for about 5 minutes, stirring constantly, until the onion is soft and translucent. Add the tequila and cook until all the liquid has been absorbed, about 2 minutes.

Combine $^3/_4$ cup of the flour, the baking powder, salt, and cayenne pepper in a mixing bowl, forming a well in the center. Add the egg white, buttermilk, and sour cream. Blend with a fork until smooth. Mix in the flaked cod and the onion and garlic mixture. Add the jalapeño pepper and the cilantro and mix thoroughly. Cover and refrigerate for 20 minutes.

Preheat the oven to 500 degrees.

Spray a nonstick baking sheet large enough to accommodate 36 fish balls in a single layer (or use 2 smaller baking sheets) lightly with vegetable oil spray, spreading the oil over the surface.

Combine the remaining ¼ cup flour and the paprika on a flat plate. Put the bread crumbs on a second plate.

With fingertips dusted in the flour and paprika, form a ball from a scant tablespoon of the chilled cod mixture. Roll it in bread crumbs to coat and place on the prepared baking sheet. Repeat the process until all the fish balls are formed. Spray them with the vegetable oil spray.

Bake for 6 minutes, then shake the pan vigorously to prevent the balls from sticking. Bake for about 6 minutes more, until golden, taking care not to overcook.

YIELD—36 FISH BALLS

Fat per fish ball—0.19 g.
Calories per fish ball—26.3

Naked Crab Imperial

1 cup finely chopped white onion
(about 1 onion)

1/2 teaspoon minced garlic

1 cup finely chopped leek, white part
only (about one 12-ounce leek)

1/3 cup chopped celery

3 tablespoons water

2 slices light oatmeal bread

1 cup seeded and coarsely chopped
tomato (about 1 tomato)

1/4 cup dry sherry

8 ounces fresh crabmeat, cartilage and
shell removed

1/4 cup clam juice

1/3 cup fresh or frozen corn kernels

2 tablespoons chopped fresh flat-leaf
parsley

2 drops hot sauce

1/2 tablespoon white wine
Worcestershire sauce

1 1/2 teaspoons Dijon-style mustard

1/8 teaspoon freshly ground
black pepper

Preheat the oven to 375 degrees.

Combine the onion, garlic, leek, celery, and water over medium heat in a nonstick frying pan. Sauté for about 5 minutes, stirring occasionally.

Toast and crumb the bread.

When the onion and leek are soft and translucent, add the tomato and sherry. Raise the heat to high and bring to a boil. Cook for 3 to 4 minutes, stirring constantly, until all the liquid has been absorbed.

Reduce the heat to low and stir in the crabmeat, clam juice, corn, parsley, hot sauce, Worcestershire sauce, mustard, and pepper. Cook for 2 to 3 minutes more, until the clam juice has evaporated.

Divide the mixture evenly among 6 individual ramekins or scallop shells and sprinkle with the bread crumbs. Place on a baking sheet and bake for 12 to 15 minutes, until bubbly.

YIELD—6 SERVINGS
Fat per serving—0.89 g.
Calories per serving—96.5

Crab and Cucumber Zingers

6 ounces cucumber, peeled and cut into twelve ½-inch slices

1 tablespoon finely chopped fresh cilantro

2 tablespoons reduced-sodium soy sauce

2 tablespoons rice vinegar

¾ teaspoon sugar

⅜ teaspoon white pepper

One 6-ounce can crabmeat, drained and picked over

Paprika for garnish (optional)

Carefully hollow out a shallow well in each cucumber slice, taking care to leave the bottoms intact.

In a mixing bowl, combine the cilantro, soy sauce, vinegar, sugar, and white pepper. Add the crabmeat and mix thoroughly.

Mound a tablespoon of the mixture into each cucumber. Dust, if desired, with paprika.

YIELD—12 STUFFED CUCUMBER SLICES

Fat per slice—0.20 g.
Calories per slice—18.5

Hot and spicy aficionados will love 'em. And there's no need to reach for a chaser—these flavor-packed morsels come with their own cooling cucumber base.

Odds are you will have all the ingredients on hand already when the doorbell rings unexpectedly.

Baby Shrimp on Artichoke Bottoms

12 canned artichoke bottoms (two 14-ounce cans), rinsed and drained

2 tablespoons plus 1 teaspoon freshly squeezed lemon juice

1/2 cup nonfat ricotta cheese

1 tablespoon chopped fresh tarragon, or 1 teaspoon dried

1 tablespoon Dijon-style mustard

3/4 teaspoon white wine vinegar

One 4 1/2-ounce can baby shrimp, rinsed and drained

1 tablespoon freshly grated Parmesan cheese

Preheat the broiler and line a cookie sheet with aluminum foil.

With a very sharp knife, trim the tough outer leaves off the sides of the artichoke bottoms. Put 2 tablespoons of the lemon juice in a small bowl. Toss the artichoke bottoms in the juice and place on the prepared cookie sheet, wells up.

Combine the ricotta cheese, tarragon, and mustard in a blender. With the machine running at the lowest speed, add the remaining 1 teaspoon of lemon juice. Turn the machine off and scrape the mixture from the sides of the bowl back into the bottom, using a rubber spatula. Turn on at low speed, add the vinegar, and continue to blend for 30 seconds. Scrape down the sides of the bowl again and then blend for 20 seconds more, until smooth. Scrape the mixture into a bowl, add the shrimp, and mix well.

Place a rounded tablespoonful of the mixture in the well of each artichoke bottom and dust each with 1/4 teaspoon of the grated Parmesan cheese. Broil for 2 to 3 minutes, until a light, crusty brown on top. Transfer to a platter and serve immediately.

Yield—12 stuffed artichoke bottoms

Fat per artichoke bottom—0.55 g.
Calories per artichoke bottom—36.3

Baked Clams

4 cherrystone clams

½ tablespoon minced garlic
  (about 2 cloves)

½ tablespoon chopped shallot

2 tablespoons finely diced red bell
  pepper

2 tablespoons chopped fresh
  flat-leaf parsley

¼ teaspoon dried thyme

¼ teaspoon dried oregano

¼ cup homemade bread crumbs
  (see Pantry)

1 tablespoon Sambuca liqueur

1 teaspoon freshly grated
  Parmesan cheese

8 lemon wedges

Preheat the oven to 425 degrees.

To shuck the clams, hold by the hinge side with a towel and pry open with a small, sharp knife. Remove and quarter each clam. Put 2 quarters into each of the 8 half shells and place the shells on a baking sheet.

Combine all the other ingredients except the Parmesan cheese and lemon wedges in a bowl and mix well. Put 2½ teaspoons of the mixture onto each shell and top with ⅛ teaspoon of the Parmesan cheese.

Bake in the oven for 5 minutes. Turn on the broiler, position the clams 6 inches from the heat source, and broil until the cheese browns, about 2 minutes.

Serve with the lemon wedges.

YIELD—8 STUFFED CLAMS

Fat per clam—0.23 g.
Calories per clam—23.2

Clams are easier to shuck when very cold. Freezing the clams for about 10 minutes should produce a small opening in the shell, into which a knife can be inserted easily. If you have them shucked at the fish market, be sure to retain the shells.

Crispy Fish and Winter Squash Cakes with Corn Sauce

1 medium carrot, peeled and cut into large chunks

1 small yellow onion, quartered

6 whole black peppercorns

2 cups water

2 cups dry white wine

1 pound fresh cod fillet

1 1/2 pounds yellow acorn squash, peeled and cut into 3/4-inch cubes (about 4 cups)

1 tablespoon plain nonfat yogurt

2 large eggs, whites only

1/4 teaspoon grated nutmeg

1/4 teaspoon dried thyme

1/4 teaspoon salt

1/8 teaspoon freshly ground black pepper

2 1/2 cups homemade bread crumbs (see Pantry)

Light vegetable oil cooking spray

CREAMY CORN SAUCE:

1 1/4 cups fresh or frozen corn kernels

1/2 cup Chicken Stock (page 6)

1/4 cup evaporated skim milk

Snipped fresh chives for garnish

Combine the carrot, onion, peppercorns, water, and wine in a large, deep-sided nonstick frying pan. Bring to a boil. Reduce the heat to medium-low, cover, and simmer for 10 minutes. Add the cod. Bring back to a simmer, cover, and poach for about 20 minutes, until the fish is flaky.

Meanwhile, bring a large saucepan of water to a boil. Add the squash cubes and cook, uncovered, over high heat for 15 to 20 minutes, until fork tender. Drain in a colander, shaking out any excess water.

When the cod is done poaching, remove the pan from the heat and set aside, covered, for 5 minutes. Remove the fish, drain, and flake.

Puree the squash to a smooth consistency in a food processor or blender. Transfer to a large mixing bowl. Add the cod, yogurt, egg whites, seasonings, and 1 1/2 cups of the bread crumbs. Mix until thoroughly combined. Cover and refrigerate for 30 minutes.

Spray a large nonstick baking sheet once lightly with the vegetable oil spray.

Using 1/4 cup of the fish and squash mixture for each, form 12 cakes about 3 inches across and 1/2 inch high. Coat with the remaining bread crumbs, place on the prepared baking sheet, cover, and refrigerate for 10 minutes.

For the sauce, bring 1 cup of the corn and the chicken stock to a boil in a small saucepan over medium heat. Reduce the heat to medium-low and simmer for 15 to 20 minutes, uncovered, until the corn can be mashed easily with a fork. Puree until smooth in a food processor or blender and set aside.

Preheat the oven to 500 degrees.

Uncover the baking sheet and spray the cakes with vegetable oil spray. Bake for 10 minutes on the bottom rack of the oven, spray the cakes again with vegetable oil spray, and bake for about 10 minutes more, until golden.

While the cakes are baking, reheat the corn puree over low heat just until it begins to give off steam. Whisk in the evaporated skim milk and the remaining corn kernels and cook for 1 to 2 minutes more, until thoroughly heated. Garnish with the chives.

Plate the cakes individually and drizzle with corn sauce.

YIELD—12 FISH CAKES

Fat per fish cake (including sauce)—0.89 g.
Calories per fish cake (including sauce)—94.3

Catfish Lunettes with Lime Sauce

6 ounces catfish fillet

1 scallion, white and light green parts only, cut into chunks

1 large egg, white only

1/4 cup evaporated skim milk

1/8 teaspoon grated nutmeg

1/4 teaspoon salt

1/8 teaspoon white pepper

24 round won ton wrappers

LIME SAUCE:

1 tablespoon arrowroot

5 tablespoons evaporated skim milk

2/3 cup Vegetable Stock (page 7)

1/4 teaspoon grated nutmeg

2 tablespoons freshly squeezed lime juice

1/4 teaspoon lime zest

Combine the catfish, scallion, egg white, evaporated skim milk, nutmeg, salt, and white pepper in the bowl of a food processor. Process until the mixture is fully incorporated and smooth, about 1 minute.

Mound 1/2 tablespoon of the mixture in the center of each won ton skin. Moisten the perimeter of the circle with water, fold in half, press closed, and crimp the outer edge with the tines of a fork.

Put a large pot of water up to boil; salt if desired.

For the sauce, in a small bowl, mix the arrowroot and the skim milk thoroughly with a fork. Set aside.

When the water is boiling, gently add the lunettes and boil until they rise to the top, about 2 minutes.

Combine the vegetable stock and the nutmeg in a small saucepan over medium heat. Cook for 2 minutes. Add the lime juice and zest. While whisking, slowly add the arrowroot and evaporated milk mixture.

Cook for 30 seconds to 1 minute more, whisking constantly, until thickened.

Arrange 3 lunettes on each plate and drizzle with the sauce.

YIELD—8 SERVINGS

Fat per serving (including sauce)—0.98 g.
Calories per serving (including sauce)—116.8

Crab Spring Rolls with Hoisin Dipping Sauce

8 spring roll wrappers

2 ounces rice stick noodles, broken into 4-inch lengths

4 ounces fresh or canned crabmeat, cartilage and shell removed

16 sprigs fresh watercress

2 ounces mung beans

16 leaves fresh basil

HOISIN DIPPING SAUCE:

1 tablespoon hoisin sauce

$1/2$ tablespoon rice vinegar

Put the spring roll wrappers into a large bowl, cover with water, and set aside to soak for 5 minutes.

Bring a medium saucepan three quarters filled with water to a boil. Add the noodles and boil for 3 minutes. Remove to a colander immediately and rinse with cold running water for 15 seconds.

Remove a wrapper from the bowl. Place 1 tablespoon of crabmeat across the middle, leaving a 1-inch border at each end. Place the leaves from 2 sprigs of watercress on top, discarding the thick stems. Layer 1 tablespoon of the mung beans, a handful of the rice stick noodles, and 2 basil leaves on top. Roll up the wrapper to seal. Repeat the process to prepare the remaining spring rolls.

For the dipping sauce, mix the hoisin sauce and vinegar well. Serve alongside the spring rolls.

YIELD—8 SPRING ROLLS

Fat per spring roll (including dipping sauce)—0.32 g.
Calories per spring roll (including dipping sauce)—131.1

Vegetables

Vidalia Onion Tart Garnished with Pepper Strips

2 pounds Vidalia onions (about 2 large
  onions), cut in half lengthwise and
  very thinly sliced

3 tablespoons water

6 sheets phyllo dough

1/4 cup Vegetable Stock (page 7)

1/2 tablespoon Dijon-style mustard

2 teaspoons chopped fresh thyme,
  or 3/4 teaspoon dried

1 red bell pepper, roasted (see Pantry),
  cut into very thin strips

Combine the onion and water in a large, deep-sided nonstick frying pan over medium heat. Cook until the onion begins to give off an aroma and turn translucent, about 3 minutes. Stir, cover, and reduce the heat to low. Cook for about 50 minutes, stirring occasionally, until the onion is very tender and a light caramel color.

Meanwhile, lay a sheet of phyllo dough onto a large nonstick baking sheet (the phyllo will overlap the rim a bit). Paint with vegetable stock. Lay 5 more sheets directly on top, painting between the layers with vegetable stock. Paint the top with the mustard.

Preheat the oven to 375 degrees.

When the onions are done, stir in the thyme. Spread over the prepared layers of phyllo dough. Bake for about 25 minutes, until browned.

Cut the tart into 12 squares with a pizza cutter and scatter the roasted red pepper on top.

YIELD—12 SQUARES

Fat per square—0.46 g.

Calories per square—63.2

Sweet Vidalia onions are spread on a paper-thin phyllo crust, simply seasoned with mustard and thyme, and splashed with roasted peppers. Serve on a buffet or individual plates. The tart makes 12 very generous portions and the yield can be doubled easily.

Cold Roasted Vegetable Lasagna

1 small white onion (about 4 ounces), quartered

2 shallots, peeled

2 cloves garlic, peeled

1 fennel bulb (about 1 pound), white part only, quartered

6 plum tomatoes (about 1 pound), cored and seeded

1/2 cup dry white wine

1 tablespoon Pernod or Sambuca liqueur

2 tablespoons chopped fresh basil

1 teaspoon chopped fresh marjoram

2 teaspoons chopped fresh thyme

Light vegetable oil cooking spray

2 yellow squash (about 1 pound), peeled and sliced lengthwise

1 small eggplant (about 1 pound), peeled and sliced lengthwise

2 yellow bell peppers (about 1 pound), trimmed and sliced lengthwise

2 large red tomatoes (about 1 pound), cored and sliced lengthwise

1 recipe Pasta (page 8), prepared through kneading

Preheat the oven to 350 degrees.

Combine the onion, shallots, garlic, fennel, and plum tomatoes in a food processor and chop. Transfer to a nonstick frying pan and add the wine. Cook over medium heat for 5 to 7 minutes, stirring constantly, until almost all the liquid has been absorbed. Stir in the liqueur and herbs. Remove the sauce from the heat and set aside.

Spray 2 large nonstick baking sheets lightly with vegetable oil spray and spread the oil over the surface. Arrange the squash, eggplant, bell peppers, and tomatoes on the sheets in a single layer. Bake for 10 minutes. Turn the vegetables over and bake for 10 minutes more. Remove from the oven and allow to cool.

Put a large pot of water up to boil.

Cut the pasta dough into 4 equal pieces. Flour the rollers of a pasta machine. Put the first piece of dough through the largest opening 3 times, folding the dough in half after each time through. Then put the dough through each successively smaller opening except the 2 smallest. Repeat the process for the remaining 3 pieces of dough.

Boil the dough, one sheet at a time, for 2 minutes. Place in a colander, drain, and hold briefly under cold running water to cool.

Lay a sheet of pasta on the bottom of a $15^3/4$- × $10^1/2$- × 2-inch lasagna pan, trimming the pasta if necessary to fit flat. Spread $^1/3$ cup of the tomato sauce over the pasta. Place the roasted squash on top in a single layer. Add a second sheet of pasta and spread with another $^1/3$ cup of sauce. Layer the roasted eggplant, the third sheet of pasta, and another $^1/3$ cup of sauce. Layer the roasted bell pepper. Place the last sheet of pasta over the pepper and top with a layer of tomato.

Cover and refrigerate. Serve cold, cut into twelve $3^1/2$-inch squares.

YIELD—12 SERVINGS

Fat per serving—0.73 g.
Calories per serving—137.1

Roasted Garlic Potatoes with Herbs in Parchment Packets

1 pound new red potatoes (unpeeled), sliced

$^{1}/_{4}$ teaspoon salt

$^{1}/_{8}$ teaspoon freshly ground black pepper

18 cloves garlic, peeled

6 fresh sage leaves

6 sprigs fresh rosemary (about 2 inches each)

Preheat the oven to 375 degrees.

Combine the potatoes, salt, and pepper in a large bowl. Mix and set aside.

Cut six 8- × 12-inch rectangles of baker's parchment. Fold each in half crosswise, crease the parchment to form a seam, and open. Put $^{1}/_{2}$ cup of the seasoned potatoes in the center of each packet, along the seam. Add 3 cloves of garlic, 1 sage leaf, and 1 sprig of rosemary.

To seal the packets, grasp both ends of the parchment opposite the inner seam and fold down about $^{1}/_{4}$ inch. Fold in the sides and fold the corners over to secure closed.

Place the packets on a baking sheet and bake for about 30 minutes, until a toothpick can be inserted easily into the potatoes. Slit the parchment packets open just before serving.

YIELD—6 SERVINGS

Fat per serving—0.08 g.
Calories per serving—56.9

Firecracker Fried Rice

1 teaspoon reduced-sodium
   soy sauce

1 tablespoon dry sherry

2 tablespoons water

1/2 teaspoon light corn syrup

Light vegetable oil cooking spray

1 cup seeded and chopped yellow bell
   pepper (about 1 pepper)

1/4 cup minced scallions (2–3 scallions)

1 cup frozen peas, thawed

2 cups cold cooked rice,
   grains separated

Preheat a wok over high heat.

Combine the soy sauce, sherry, water, and corn syrup in a bowl, mix thoroughly, and set aside.

Spray the hot wok twice with the vegetable oil spray. Put the pepper and scallion into the wok, and stir-fry for 30 seconds. Add the peas and rice and cook for 2 minutes more, still stirring constantly. Add the soy sauce mixture and toss to coat.

YIELD—4 SERVINGS

Fat per serving—0.61 g.
Calories per serving—115.9

This home-style Chinese dish is distinctively white, a novel contrast to the darker restaurant versions. For our healthy adaptation, we stir-fry without the typical ration of oil, use less soy sauce, and avoid the common addition of pork. We also skip the superfluous bits of egg; here, flecks of yellow bell pepper add a similar splash of color, imparting a bit of sweetness as well.

Stuffed Mushrooms

8 large white button mushrooms
(about 8 ounces)

Light vegetable oil cooking spray

1 slice light whole wheat bread,
freshly toasted

2 tablespoons chopped fresh
flat-leaf parsley

2 teaspoons chopped garlic
(2–3 cloves)

4 teaspoons brandy

5 teaspoons water

1/4 teaspoon salt

1/8 teaspoon freshly ground
black pepper

Preheat the broiler.

Clean and stem the mushrooms. Cut the stems into chunks and reserve.

Spray a glass baking dish once lightly with the vegetable oil spray. Place the mushrooms in the dish, stem side down. Broil for 3 to 4 minutes, until lightly browned. Remove and set aside, leaving the broiler on.

Rip the toast into chunks and place it in the bowl of a food processor. Add the parsley and the reserved mushroom stems. Process to a fine consistency.

Turn the mixture into a bowl. Stir in the garlic, brandy, and water. Add the salt and pepper and combine thoroughly. Turn the mushrooms over and stuff about 1 tablespoon into each. Broil for 5 to 6 minutes, until browned.

Serve hot or room temperature.

YIELD—8 STUFFED MUSHROOMS

Fat per mushroom—0.22 g.

Calories per mushroom—19.7

Potato and Pepper Frittata

One 8-ounce red potato, peeled and
    cut into thin rounds

One 4-ounce white onion, peeled and
    cut into half-rounds

One 6-ounce red bell pepper, cored,
    seeded, and thinly sliced

2 tablespoons water

1 cup nonfat liquid egg substitute

$1/2$ cup buttermilk

2 tablespoons skim milk

1 teaspoon dried thyme

$1/4$ teaspoon salt

$1/4$ teaspoon freshly ground black
    pepper

Light vegetable oil cooking spray

Preheat the oven to 325 degrees.

Preheat a large nonstick frying pan over medium heat. Add the potato, onion, bell pepper, and water. Cook for about 5 minutes, stirring constantly, until the potato is fork tender.

Combine the egg substitute, buttermilk, and skim milk in a large mixing bowl and whisk well. Add the seasonings. Mix in the potato mixture.

Preheat a 9-inch cast-iron skillet over high heat. Spray once with the vegetable oil spray and pour in the batter. Place in the oven and bake for about 35 minutes, until slightly browned with firm edges.

Remove the frittata from the oven and cool for a few minutes before slicing into 8 wedges. Serve warm or at room temperature.

YIELD—8 SERVINGS

Fat per serving—0.33 g.
Calories per serving—49.4

This is our version of a traditional dish that graces tapas bars throughout Spain. It can also be served with a salad for lunch or as a light main course.

Pinto Bean Cakes in Ancho Chile Sauce

One 15-ounce can pinto beans, rinsed and drained

¹/₂ cup seeded and diced tomato (about 1 small tomato)

¹/₃ cup chopped white onion

¹/₄ teaspoon minced garlic

¹/₃ cup fresh or frozen corn kernels

1 tablespoon finely chopped fresh cilantro

1 teaspoon ground cumin

¹/₂ teaspoon dried oregano

¹/₂ teaspoon salt

1 tablespoon nonfat sour cream

4 drops hot sauce

Light vegetable oil cooking spray

2 tablespoons cornmeal

ANCHO CHILE SAUCE:

3 large dried ancho chile peppers

3 cups boiling water

¹/₄ teaspoon minced garlic

1 teaspoon dried oregano

¹/₄ cup Vegetable Stock (page 7)

Combine the chiles for the sauce and the boiling water in a bowl, cover tightly, and set aside.

Put the pinto beans into a large bowl. Mash to a crumbly consistency with a potato masher or fork, leaving a few beans whole. Add the tomato, onion, garlic, corn, cilantro, cumin, oregano, salt, sour cream, and hot sauce. Mix thoroughly.

Spray a nonstick baking sheet once lightly with the vegetable oil spray and spread the oil over the surface. Using a scant ¹/₄ cup of the mixture for each, form 8 cakes. Roll the cakes in the cornmeal to coat lightly and place on the sheet. Cover and refrigerate for at least 30 minutes before baking.

Preheat the oven to 500 degrees.

Bake the bean cakes for 10 minutes, turn them over, and bake for about 10 minutes more. Allow to cool a bit before serving.

For the sauce, remove the chile peppers from the soaking liquid. Stem and break them open. Core, seed, and devein. Transfer to the bowl of a food processor. Strain ½ cup of the soaking liquid into the bowl. Add the garlic, oregano, and vegetable stock and puree until smooth. Remove to a saucepan and warm over low heat, stirring occasionally, for about 3 minutes. Drizzle some of the sauce over each cake.

YIELD—8 BEAN CAKES

Fat per cake (including sauce)—0.53 g.
Calories per cake (including sauce)—72.0

Spinach Quenelles in Tomato Sauce

10 ounces fresh spinach, rinsed and stemmed

^{1}/$_4$ cup nonfat ricotta cheese

2 tablespoons nonfat liquid egg substitute

1 tablespoon finely chopped fresh dill

^{1}/$_8$ teaspoon freshly grated nutmeg

^{1}/$_4$ teaspoon salt, plus extra to taste

^{1}/$_8$ teaspoon freshly ground black pepper, plus extra to taste

^{1}/$_2$ cup all-purpose flour

TOMATO SAUCE:

One 14^1/$_2$-ounce can diced tomatoes

^{1}/$_4$ cup chopped carrot

^{1}/$_4$ cup chopped celery

^{1}/$_4$ teaspoon sugar

Steam the spinach over boiling water until wilted, about 3 minutes. Transfer to a colander, let cool a bit, and squeeze as much water as possible from the spinach. Roughly chop.

Put the ricotta into a mixing bowl. Add the liquid egg substitute and mix thoroughly with a fork. Mix in the dill, nutmeg, ^{1}/$_4$ teaspoon salt, ^{1}/$_8$ teaspoon pepper, and the spinach.

Using 1 tablespoon of the mixture for each, form into 18 firm egg-shaped quenelles. Roll in the flour to coat.

For the sauce, combine the ingredients in a small saucepan. Bring to a boil over medium heat. Reduce the heat to medium-low and simmer, uncovered, for about 20 minutes, until the mixture has thickened slightly and the carrot is soft.

Transfer to a food processor or blender and puree to a smooth consistency. Return to the saucepan and keep warm over low heat.

Bring a large, deep-sided nonstick frying pan half-filled with water to a boil over high heat. Reduce the heat to medium-low. Gently add the quenelles, a few at a time, and cook until they rise to the surface, about 2 minutes.

Serve 3 quenelles on each of 6 plates and top each serving with tomato sauce. Add salt and pepper to taste.

Fat per serving (including sauce)—0.24 g.
Calories per serving (including sauce)—66.5

Salads

Rock Shrimp, Scallop, and Squid Ceviche in Radicchio Boats

1 cup dry white wine

1 cup water

3 whole sprigs plus $1/2$ cup chopped
   fresh cilantro

2 large cleaned squid bodies (about
   2 ounces), cut into rings

4 ounces sea scallops, quartered

4 ounces rock shrimp, shelled

2 tomatoes (about 12 ounces), cored,
   seeded, and cut into $1/2$-inch cubes
   (about 2 cups)

1 cup coarsely chopped red onion
   (about 1 small onion)

1 cup chopped red bell pepper
   (about 1 pepper)

1 cup frozen corn kernels, thawed

2 kiwis (about 6 ounces), peeled and
   cut into $1/4$-inch cubes (about 1 cup)

$1/2$ tablespoon minced garlic
   (about 2 cloves)

$1/2$ tablespoon seeded, deveined, and
   finely chopped jalapeño pepper

7 tablespoons freshly squeezed
   lime juice

8 leaves radicchio

Combine the wine, water, and whole sprigs of cilantro in a nonstick frying pan. Bring to a boil over high heat, reduce the heat to medium, and simmer, uncovered, for 5 minutes. Add the squid and cook for 5 minutes. Add the scallops and cook for another 2 minutes. Stir in the shrimp and cook for about 1 minute more, until the shrimp turn pink. Drain and transfer the seafood to a large bowl.

To the bowl, add the vegetables, kiwis, garlic, jalapeño pepper, $1/2$ cup chopped cilantro, and the lime juice. Toss to mix thoroughly.

Plate 8 individual servings, each atop a radicchio leaf, or line a salad bowl with the leaves and mound the ceviche on top.

YIELD—8 SERVINGS

Fat per serving—0.98 g.
Calories per serving—106.3

Here is a delightful blend of lightly cooked seafood in a lively dressing. Serve warm, at room temperature or chilled. Individually plated, it's a generous portion.

This stylish first course can be made easily a day in advance. Plate individual servings or arrange the terrine on a platter, atop a bed of bitter greens, for a buffet.

The terrine should be sliced with a very sharp (nonserrated) knife; a cake server will facilitate handling.

Cantaloupe and Peach Terrine with Salad of Bitter Greens

1 small ripe cantaloupe (about 2 pounds), peeled, seeded, and cut into $1/2$-inch cubes (about 2 cups)

4 ounces watercress, stems removed

Freshly ground black pepper to taste

3 large ripe peaches (about 1 pound), peeled, stoned, and thinly sliced (about 2 cups)

4 ounces arugula, stems removed

$1 1/4$ cups water

2 packets unflavored gelatin

$1/4$ cup Madeira wine

1 pound mixed bitter salad greens

1 cup fresh raspberries

DRESSING:

$1 3/4$ cups Madeira wine

$1/4$ cup raspberry vinegar

2 tablespoons sugar

Line a $9 1/4$-inch loaf pan with plastic wrap, leaving enough overlap to seal the terrine after the pan has been filled.

Arrange half the cantaloupe cubes in the bottom of the prepared loaf pan. Layer half of the watercress over the melon and dust with black pepper, then add half of the peach slices. Spread half of the arugula on top of the peaches and once again dust with black pepper. Add a layer of the remaining cantaloupe cubes, then the remaining watercress, pepper to taste, and finally the remaining peach slices.

Bring the water to a boil in a small saucepan over medium heat. Stir in the gelatin and remove the pan from the heat. Continue to stir until the gelatin has dissolved totally. Stir in the wine. Pour the mixture over the contents of the loaf pan and top with the remaining arugula.

Close the plastic wrap over the pan and top with an additional layer of doubled plastic wrap to seal. Put the loaf pan onto a large plate and weigh the pan down with another loaf pan of the same size filled with water, bags of dried beans, or anything else sufficiently heavy, or with a brick. Refrigerate for at least 3 hours to allow the aspic to form and the terrine to set.

For the dressing, combine all the ingredients in a small saucepan. Bring to a boil over high heat and continue to boil for 10 to 12 minutes, until reduced by half, to about 1 cup. Cool to room temperature and chill.

To unmold the terrine, open the plastic wrap, put a serving plate upside down on top of the loaf pan, flip, and remove the plastic. Cut into 8 equal slices with a sharp knife.

Line each of 8 chilled salad plates with 1 cup of the bitter greens. Place a slice of terrine on each plate, garnish with raspberries, and drizzle with the dressing.

YIELD—8 SERVINGS

Fat per serving (including dressing)—0.37 g.
Calories per serving (including dressing)—119.2

Eggplant Crostini
with Warm Tomato Salad

Light vegetable oil cooking spray

2 baby white or purple eggplant
(about 12 ounces), sliced into a
total of eighteen 1/4-inch rounds

2 red tomatoes (about 1 pound), cored

2 yellow tomatoes (about 1 pound),
cored

32 leaves fresh basil, rinsed and dried

2 teaspoons balsamic vinegar

Salt and freshly ground black pepper
to taste

6 teaspoons shredded nonfat
mozzarella cheese

Preheat the oven to 450 degrees.

Spray a nonstick baking pan once lightly with the vegetable oil spray and smooth the oil evenly over the surface. Place the eggplant rounds on the pan in a single layer and spray once again lightly. Bake for 15 minutes. Remove the pan from the oven and raise the temperature to preheat the broiler.

Cut the tomatoes into 1/2-inch cubes and place them in a bowl. (You should have about 4 cups of cubed tomatoes.) Slice the basil leaves crosswise and add to the tomatoes. Add the vinegar and toss well to mix.

Top each of the eggplant rounds with 1 tablespoon of the tomato salad. Salt and pepper to taste. Sprinkle 1 teaspoon of the shredded mozzarella cheese over each round. Broil for about 1 minute, just until the cheese has melted and lightly browned.

YIELD—18 EGGPLANT CROSTINI

Fat per crostini—0.22 g.

Calories per crostini—17.0

Garlic-Infused Carrot Salad

1 pound carrots, peeled

3/4 teaspoon chopped garlic
(about 1 clove)

3 tablespoons honey

2 tablespoons freshly squeezed
lemon juice

3 tablespoons chopped fresh mint

Shred the carrots by hand or in a food processor fitted with the fine grating disc. Put into a serving bowl.

In a small bowl, whisk together the garlic, honey, and lemon juice. Pour over the carrots, add the mint, toss well to mix, and serve.

YIELD—6 SERVINGS

Fat per serving—0.17 g.
Calories per serving—62.6

Not at all like Mom's carrot and raisin salad, this is a sophisticated blend of sweet and savory that tantalizes the taste buds and defies comparison.

Black Bean, Corn, and Jicama Salad

3 cups water

6 ounces dried black beans (about ³/₄ cup), rinsed and picked over

1 large ear of corn in husk

³/₄ cup peeled and finely diced jicama

¹/₂ cup chopped red onion

1 tablespoon seeded, deveined, and chopped jalapeño pepper

2 tablespoons finely chopped fresh cilantro

1 teaspoon dried oregano

1 cup shredded red-leaf lettuce

DRESSING:

3 tablespoons freshly squeezed lime juice

¹/₂ tablespoon minced garlic (about 2 cloves)

2 tablespoons freshly squeezed orange juice

¹/₂ tablespoon light corn syrup

Bring the water to a boil in a large saucepan. Add the beans, bring back to a boil, and boil for 5 minutes. Cover, remove from the heat, and set aside for 1 hour.

Drain, refill the pan with water, and bring back to a boil over high heat. Boil for about 30 minutes, until the beans are fork tender. Drain well and transfer the beans to a large serving bowl.

Put the corn in its husk into a microwave oven. Cook at full power for 1 minute, turn the ear over, and microwave for 1 minute more. Carefully remove the husk and silk, cut the corn from the ear, and add to the bowl with the beans. Add the remaining ingredients and toss.

For the dressing, whisk together all the ingredients in a small bowl. Pour over the salad, toss to mix well, cover, and refrigerate for at least 1 hour before serving.

YIELD—6 SERVINGS
Fat per serving (including dressing)—0.73 g.
Calories per serving (including dressing)—137.5

Tricolor Pasta Salad
with Tarragon Vinaigrette

4 ounces snow peas, trimmed and cut
 into bite-size pieces

8 ounces cherry tomatoes, quartered

3 cups cooked tricolor rotini

TARRAGON VINAIGRETTE:

1/2 cup plain nonfat yogurt

1/2 tablespoon white wine vinegar

1 teaspoon Dijon-style mustard

1 teaspoon chopped fresh tarragon

3/4 teaspoon chopped fresh chives

1/8 teaspoon salt

1/8 teaspoon freshly ground
 black pepper

Bring a small saucepan of water to a boil. Add the snow peas, blanch for 20 seconds, remove immediately to a colander, and rinse with cold running water for 15 seconds.

Transfer to a serving bowl and add the tomatoes and the cooked rotini.

For the dressing, combine the ingredients in a bowl and blend thoroughly. Pour over the pasta salad, toss to mix, cover, and refrigerate for at least 30 minutes before serving.

YIELD—6 SERVINGS

Fat per serving (including dressing)—0.85 g.
Calories per serving (including dressing)—171.5

We think pasta salad is one of the best culinary trends of recent years, and can't understand why such an inherently flavorful and healthy dish is so often ruined by overdressing. Here, a colorful array of rotini, blanched snow peas, and fresh cherry tomatoes are presented in a minimal vinaigrette spiked with aromatic fresh tarragon.

Grapefruit, Cucumber, and Fennel Salad

2 ruby grapefruit (about 1½ pounds)

10 ounces English (seedless) cucumber

1 fennel bulb (about 12 ounces)

2 Bosc pears (about 12 ounces)

DRESSING:

½ cup honey

2 tablespoons freshly squeezed orange juice

2 tablespoons freshly squeezed lemon juice

1 tablespoon finely chopped fresh basil

Peel, seed, and separate the grapefruit sections, removing the membranes.

Peel and cube the cucumber (seed if not using an English, or hot-house, cucumber).

Cut the fennel bulb in half and thinly slice lengthwise.

Cut the pears in half, core, and thinly slice lengthwise.

For the dressing, whisk together the ingredients in a small bowl. Pour the dressing over the salad and toss. Cover and refrigerate for 30 minutes before serving.

YIELD—6 SERVINGS

Fat per serving (including dressing)—0.41 g.
Calories per serving (including dressing)—151.1

Spicy Chicken Salad

2 cups water

8 whole black peppercorns

10 ounces skinless, boneless chicken
    breast

1/4 cup reduced-sodium soy sauce

3 tablespoons honey

1/2 teaspoon minced garlic

1/3 cup finely chopped white onion

1/2 teaspoon freshly grated ginger

1/8 teaspoon red pepper flakes

4 cups chopped romaine lettuce
    (about 1 head)

1/2 cup sliced water chestnuts

1/2 cup canned whole baby corn spears,
    rinsed and drained

4 ounces red bell pepper, cored, seeded,
    and sliced in rounds for garnish

Combine the water and peppercorns in a large, deep-sided nonstick frying pan and bring to a boil. Add the chicken, cover, and cook over medium heat for 20 minutes.

Meanwhile, combine the soy sauce, honey, and garlic in a small bowl. Mix and set aside.

When the chicken is done, remove the pan from the heat and let sit, covered, for 5 minutes. Transfer the chicken to a plate and allow it to cool.

Preheat a small nonstick frying pan over a medium heat. Add the onion, ginger, and red pepper flakes. Cook for 30 seconds, stirring constantly. Remove from the heat and let cool.

Shred the chicken. Combine in a bowl with the lettuce, water chestnuts, and corn.

Pour the reserved soy and honey mixture into the small frying pan with the onion and ginger. Stir to combine thoroughly. Pour over the chicken salad and toss.

Garnish with the bell pepper rings.

YIELD—6 SERVINGS

Fat per serving—0.96 g.
Calories per serving—116.5

It's amazing what happens to chicken salad when you strip away the mounds of tasteless mayonnaise and the restrictive confines of a sandwich!
    This robust rendition has become a household favorite and the basis for ceaseless variation, depending upon mood. Kevin has even been known to add a few drops of hot sauce to the already volatile mixture.

Salsas, Dips, AND Relishes

Tomatillo Salsa
with Baked Tortilla Chips

6 tomatillos (about 12 ounces), husked and stemmed

½ cup chopped white onion

3 tablespoons seeded, deveined, and chopped jalapeño pepper (about 1 large pepper)

2 tablespoons finely chopped fresh cilantro

1 teaspoon minced garlic

2 tablespoons freshly squeezed lime juice

½ teaspoon light corn syrup

½ teaspoon dried tarragon

¼ teaspoon salt

Pinch of freshly ground black pepper

Six 6-inch corn tortillas

In this recipe, just a touch of light corn syrup lends the viscosity of oil and tempers the pungent mixture of onion, garlic, and lime.

Roughly chop the tomatillos and place them in a large mixing bowl. Add the onion, jalapeño pepper, cilantro, and garlic. Mix thoroughly.

In a small bowl, combine the lime juice, corn syrup, tarragon, salt, and black pepper. Whisk and pour over the tomatillo mixture. Serve room temperature or cover and chill.

For the tortilla chips, preheat the oven to 375 degrees and put a sheet of aluminum foil on the middle rack.

Cut each tortilla into 6 triangular chips. Place the triangles on the foil paper and bake for about 5 minutes, until toasted.

YIELD—ABOUT 2⅓ CUPS SALSA AND 36 TORTILLA CHIPS

Fat per tablespoon of salsa—0.06 g.; per chip—0.04 g.

Calories per tablespoon of salsa—4.1; per chip—4.2

We highly recommend that you use fresh corn for this lively salsa, which pairs well with Baked Tortilla Chips (page 85) or alongside the Chicken Tamales (page 18) or Turkey and Leek Rolls (page 23). It's best very fresh; prepare, chill briefly, and serve immediately.

Corn Salsa

1 cup corn kernels

$^{1}/_{2}$ cup diced red bell pepper

$^{1}/_{4}$ cup chopped scallions (about 3 scallions)

1 tablespoon seeded, deveined, and diced jalapeño pepper

1 tablespoon finely chopped fresh cilantro

$^{1}/_{2}$ tablespoon chopped fresh thyme

1 tablespoon white balsamic vinegar

1 tablespoon freshly squeezed lime juice

$^{1}/_{2}$ tablespoon white wine vinegar

Combine all the ingredients in a bowl and mix thoroughly. Cover and chill.

YIELD—ABOUT 1$^{1}/_{2}$ CUPS

Fat per tablespoon—0.09 g.

Calories per tablespoon—6.6

Black Bean Dip

One 15-ounce can black beans,
  rinsed and drained

2 tablespoons finely chopped carrot

2 tablespoons finely chopped celery

1/2 tablespoon minced garlic
  (about 2 cloves)

1/4 cup plain nonfat yogurt

1 tablespoon chopped fresh cilantro,
  plus additional for garnish

1 teaspoon dried oregano

1 teaspoon ground cumin

1/2 teaspoon ground coriander

1/4 teaspoon salt

Put half the beans into a large mixing bowl and mash roughly with a fork.
Add the rest of the beans, along with the remaining ingredients. Mix
thoroughly. Cover and chill.

Garnish with the additional cilantro.

YIELD—ABOUT 2 1/2 CUPS

Fat per tablespoon—0.08 g.

Calories per tablespoon—15.6

Spicy, yes—but flecked with cool bits of carrot and celery and sultry hints of cilantro. Serve with Baked Tortilla Chips (page 85) or Crispy Potato Skins (page 91).

Eggplant Caviar

1 eggplant (about 1¼ pounds)

2 cloves garlic, peeled

1 teaspoon reduced-sodium soy sauce

1 tablespoon freshly squeezed lemon juice

¾ cup chopped tomato

2 tablespoons diced scallion, white and light green parts only (about 1 large scallion)

2 tablespoons finely chopped fresh flat-leaf parsley

1 tablespoon chopped fresh basil

Preheat the oven to 400 degrees.

Place the eggplant on a baking sheet lined with aluminum foil and bake for 45 minutes.

Cut in half lengthwise. As the eggplant cools, squeeze out the excess water. Scoop out the pulp, transfer it to a bowl, and mash with a fork. Press in the garlic. Add the remaining ingredients and combine well.

Cover and chill before serving.

YIELD—ABOUT 2 CUPS

Fat per tablespoon—0.03 g.

Calories per tablespoon—5.5

Cucumber Mint Dip
with Pita Chips

1 cup peeled, seeded, and coarsely grated cucumber (about 1 small cucumber)

1/4 teaspoon white pepper

2 tablespoons chopped fresh mint leaves

1 cup plain nonfat yogurt

1/4 cup finely chopped green bell pepper

1 tablespoon grated onion

Salt to taste

2 pita pockets

Squeeze excess water out of the grated cucumber and place in a mixing bowl. Add the white pepper and mint and mix well. Add the yogurt, bell pepper, onion, and salt. Combine thoroughly. Cover and chill.

Preheat the oven to 375 degrees.

Cut each pita pocket open to produce a total of 4 circles of bread. Cut each circle into 8 wedges. Arrange them in a single layer on a large (or 2 smaller) nonstick baking sheet(s). Bake the pitas for 7 to 8 minutes, until very crisp.

Serve the chips and dip together.

YIELD—ABOUT 1 1/2 CUPS DIP AND 32 TORTILLA CHIPS

Fat per tablespoon of dip—0.03 g.; per chip—0.06 g.
Calories per tablespoon of dip—6.6; per chip—9.9

Cool as the proverbial cucumber, this dip perks up a simple cold vegetable platter. We like it alongside Minted Turkey Meatballs (page 13), Spicy Baked Salt Cod Balls (page 46), and Crab and Cucumber Zingers (page 49).

Who says bean dips have to be high in fat? This is a hearty concoction tempered with a medley of delicate fresh herbs. Serve with sturdy dipping crackers or an assortment of cocktail breads.

Great Northern Bean Spread

1 1/4 cups cooked Great Northern beans

1/4 cup fresh cilantro leaves

1/4 cup fresh parsley leaves

1/4 cup fresh mint leaves

1/4 cup water

1/2 teaspoon ground cumin

1/4 teaspoon chopped garlic

3 tablespoons freshly squeezed lemon juice

Combine the beans, cilantro, parsley, and mint in the bowl of a food processor and coarsely chop. With the motor running, drizzle the water in through the feed tube. Transfer to a serving bowl and stir in the cumin, garlic, and lemon juice.

YIELD—ABOUT 1 1/4 CUPS

Fat per tablespoon—0.08 g.

Calories per tablespoon—13.6

Roasted Pepper Relish with Crispy Potato Skins

2 red bell peppers (about 14 ounces), halved, cored, seeded, and deveined

1 large jalapeño pepper, halved, cored, seeded, and deveined

2 tablespoons finely chopped fresh flat-leaf parsley

1/2 teaspoon chopped garlic

2 tablespoons freshly squeezed lemon juice

2 baking potatoes

Preheat the broiler and line the rack with aluminum foil.

Place all 3 peppers on the broiler rack, cut side down. Remove the jalapeño pepper after 3 to 4 minutes and transfer to an airtight plastic bag. Char the bell pepper for an additional 1 to 2 minutes and remove to the bag. Seal and set aside to cool for about 10 minutes. Turn the oven down to 400 degrees.

Remove the peppers from the plastic bag, rub off the skin, dice, and place in a mixing bowl. Mix in the parsley, garlic, and lemon juice. Cover and chill.

Place the potatoes on the bottom rack of the oven and bake them for 45 minutes. Remove from the oven and let cool, leaving the oven on.

Cut the potatoes in half lengthwise and scoop out most of the meat, leaving only a thin lining of potato. Quarter each half potato shell. Place the quartered shells on a baking sheet. Bake on the bottom rack of the oven for 15 minutes, turning the shells over after 7 to 8 minutes.

Serve the potato skins alongside the relish for dipping.

YIELD—ABOUT 1 CUP RELISH AND 16 POTATO SKINS

Fat per tablespoon of relish—0.06 g.; per skin—0.01 g.
Calories per tablespoon of relish—4.0; per skin—14.0

Simple to execute yet complex in flavor, this chutney literally can be made in a matter of minutes from pantry staples. We discovered the recipe by accident, but like it as well as most traditional cooked chutneys.

The chutney makes a pleasant accompaniment to Beef and Baked Potato Empanadas (page 28) or Savory Meat-Filled Pastries (page 22). Or serve it with an assortment of dried fruit.

Apple Chutney

1 cup natural unsweetened chunky-style applesauce, chilled

1 teaspoon white wine vinegar

1/4 teaspoon dried tarragon

1/4 cup seedless raisins

4 teaspoons dark brown sugar, firmly packed

1 teaspoon curry powder

Combine the applesauce and vinegar in a serving bowl. Add the tarragon, raisins, brown sugar, and curry powder. Mix thoroughly.

If not serving immediately, cover and refrigerate.

YIELD—ABOUT 1 1/2 CUPS

Fat per tablespoon—0.02 g.
Calories per tablespoon—16.7

Pastas, Sandwiches, AND Pizzas

Pasta Tossed in Roasted Red Pepper Sauce

12 sun-dried tomatoes

$1/2$ cup boiling water

1 cup sliced roasted red bell pepper (see Pantry)

2 teaspoons minced garlic (2–3 cloves)

$3/4$ cup Chicken Stock (page 6)

2 large scallions, trimmed and cut into thin rounds (about $1/2$ cup)

3 tablespoons chopped fresh basil

2 teaspoons dried oregano

$1/2$ teaspoon salt

$1/8$ teaspoon freshly ground black pepper

12 ounces Pasta (page 8), cooked (about 6 cups)

$1/2$ tablespoon freshly grated Parmesan cheese

This minimalist sauce coats the pasta with a veneer of rich stock, providing moisture, flavor, and sheen—but allowing the flecks of sun-dried tomato, roasted red pepper, and herbs to be showcased. It works perfectly with our fresh homemade pasta.

Combine the tomatoes and boiling water in a small bowl and set aside for about 15 minutes to reconstitute.

Remove the tomatoes, reserving the soaking liquid, and thinly slice.

In a large nonstick frying pan, combine the tomatoes, roasted pepper, garlic, and $1/2$ cup of the chicken stock. Cook over medium-high heat for 2 to 3 minutes, until the garlic begins to give off its aroma.

Stir in the scallions, basil, oregano, salt, pepper, and pasta. Strain in the reserved soaking liquid. Cook, stirring constantly, for 2 to 3 minutes more. Add the remaining $1/4$ cup of chicken stock and cook just until thoroughly heated and combined.

Divide among 6 pasta bowls, topping each with $1/4$ teaspoon of the Parmesan cheese.

YIELD—6 SERVINGS

Fat per serving (including sauce)—0.78 g.

Calories per serving (including sauce)—141.9

Spinach Pasta with Tomato Sauce

10 ounces fresh spinach, stems removed

1 1/2 cups all-purpose flour, plus a little extra for flouring during preparation

4 to 5 tablespoons nonfat liquid egg substitute

TOMATO SAUCE:

One 28-ounce can peeled Italian-style plum tomatoes, drained, seeded, and coarsely chopped, liquid reserved

1/2 cup diced onion

2 teaspoons finely chopped garlic (2–3 cloves)

1/4 cup finely chopped celery

1/2 cup finely chopped carrot

1 tablespoon chopped fresh basil

1/4 teaspoon freshly ground black pepper

1/4 teaspoon salt, plus 1 tablespoon for cooking the pasta

Wash, drain, and dry the spinach. Coarsely chop in a food processor. Add the flour and process until well mixed. While pulsing, add the liquid egg substitute, one tablespoon at a time, just until bits of dough the size of large peas form.

Turn the dough out onto a floured board and knead until glossy and elastic. Form into a ball, cover with plastic wrap, and set aside for 30 minutes.

Flour the rollers of a pasta machine. Divide the dough into 8 pieces and put the first piece through the largest opening on the pasta machine 3 times, folding the dough in half after each time through. Then put it through each successively smaller opening, except the smallest. Repeat the process for the remaining 7 pieces of dough. Cut the pasta into wide ribbons and allow it to dry for 20 minutes before cooking.

For the sauce, heat 5 tablespoons of the reserved tomato liquid over medium heat in a nonstick frying pan. Add the onion, garlic, celery, and carrot. Cook for about 7 minutes, stirring occasionally, until the onion and celery are soft. Stir in the tomatoes, basil, pepper, and ¼ teaspoon of the salt. Reduce the heat to low and simmer, uncovered, until the sauce thickens, about 15 minutes.

Remove the pan from the heat and let the sauce cool briefly, then transfer to a food processor and pulse to make a coarse puree. (The sauce may be made ahead and reheated.)

To cook the pasta, bring a large pot of water to a boil over high heat. Add the pasta and the remaining 1 tablespoon of salt. Cook only to the al dente stage, about 4 minutes.

Drain the pasta in a colander, transfer to a serving bowl, and toss with the sauce. Serve immediately.

YIELD—6 SERVINGS

Fat per serving (including sauce)—0.48 g.
Calories per serving (including sauce)—154.0

Tomato, Roasted Yellow Pepper, and Pimiento Crostini

2 yellow bell peppers (about 12 ounces), cut in half lengthwise, cored, seeded, and deveined

3 large tomatoes (about 1½ pounds), cored and cut into ½-inch cubes

4 pimientos, thinly sliced lengthwise

1 teaspoon seeded, deveined, and finely chopped jalapeño pepper

½ tablespoon chopped fresh thyme, or ½ teaspoon dried

⅓ cup finely chopped white onion

½ teaspoon minced garlic

2 teaspoons freshly squeezed lime juice

¼ teaspoon salt

Twelve ½-inch slices French Bread (page 9)

Preheat the broiler.

Place the bell pepper halves on aluminum foil on the broiler rack, cut side down. Broil for about 5 minutes and carefully remove from the oven, leaving the broiler on. Transfer to an airtight plastic bag and set aside to cool for about 10 minutes.

Meanwhile, combine the tomatoes, pimientos, jalapeño pepper, thyme, onion, garlic, lime juice, and salt in a large bowl and mix well.

Remove the peppers from the plastic bag, rub off the skin, cut into long strips, and add to the mixing bowl.

Toast the bread in the broiler for about 2 minutes, on one side only. Transfer to a serving plate, toasted side down. Press down on each slice with a large spoon to make a bit of a well. Mound 3 tablespoons of the salad mixture onto each slice.

YIELD—12 SERVINGS

Fat per serving—0.40 g.

Calories per serving—62.4

Provençal Fish Sandwich

2 large anchovy fillets, rinsed, drained, and finely chopped

5 medium black Mission or manzanilla olives, chopped

1 cup chopped scallions, white and light green parts only (about 2 bunches)

One 6-ounce can chunk light tuna, packed in water, drained and flaked

$^1/_8$ teaspoon freshly ground black pepper

1 tablespoon freshly squeezed lemon juice

1 large tomato (about 8 ounces), cored and thinly sliced

Sixteen $^1/_4$-inch slices French Bread (page 9)

2 red bell peppers, roasted (see Pantry), cut into thin strips

Combine the anchovies, olives, scallions, tuna, black pepper, and lemon juice in a bowl and mix well.

Lay a tomato slice on each of 8 slices of bread. Mound a scant $^1/_4$ cup of the tuna mixture over the tomato and lay about a tablespoon of roasted pepper strips on top. Add the remaining slice of bread to each, cut in half if desired, and arrange on a serving platter.

YIELD—8 SANDWICHES

Fat per sandwich—0.85 g.
Calories per sandwich—80.9

Prepared with preroasted peppers and canned tuna, this recipe turns a freshly baked loaf of French Bread into an intriguing appetizer in minutes. Sort of a tuna niçoise on a baguette, it's filling fare for the armchair mariner.

Open-Face Spinach Sandwiches on Pumpernickel

10 ounces fresh spinach, washed (but not dried), stems removed, and coarsely chopped (about 6 cups)

1/2 cup plain nonfat yogurt

1/4 cup low-fat (1%) cottage cheese

1 scallion, white and light green parts only, finely chopped

2 teaspoons chopped fresh dill, or 3/4 teaspoon dried

4 drops hot sauce

Salt to taste

1 clove garlic, peeled

16 slices cocktail pumpernickel

Paprika for garnish (optional)

Put the spinach in a microwave-safe container, cover, and microwave at full power for 1 1/2 minutes, rotating the dish after 45 seconds, or steam for about 3 minutes, until wilted.

Remove the spinach to a colander, rinse briefly under cold running water, and drain, pressing down with the back of a spoon to remove excess water.

Combine the yogurt and cottage cheese in a blender and blend at the lowest speed for about 1 minute, until the mixture is smooth. Transfer to a bowl and add the drained spinach, the scallion, dill, hot sauce, and salt. Press in the garlic.

Spread the spinach mixture onto the pumpernickel slices. Arrange the open-face sandwiches on a serving platter and dust, if desired, with paprika.

YIELD—16 SANDWICHES

Fat per sandwich—0.35 g.
Calories per sandwich—25.9

Pizza Dough

¹/₄ cup lukewarm water
(105–115 degrees on an
instant-read thermometer),
plus 1 cup cold water

¹/₂ teaspoon sugar

1 packet quick-rise yeast

3 cups all-purpose flour

¹/₃ cup semolina

¹/₂ tablespoon salt

1¹/₂ tablespoons nonfat liquid egg
substitute

Put the lukewarm water and the sugar into a small bowl. Sprinkle the yeast on top and set aside for a few minutes, until the mixture is bubbly.

Combine the flour, semolina, salt, and liquid egg substitute in the bowl of a food processor. Process for 1 minute. Scrape in the yeast mixture. Turn the machine back on and drizzle the cold water through the feed tube until a dough ball forms, then process for 1 additional minute.

Remove the dough to a lightly floured work surface. Knead 6 to 7 times. Transfer the ball to a bowl, cover with a damp towel, and set aside for 1¹/₂ hours until the dough about doubles in size.

Proceed according to specific pizza or focaccia recipe directions.

YIELD—SUFFICIENT DOUGH FOR EIGHT 4-INCH PIZZAS
OR TWO 10-INCH FOCACCIA

We use this tasty, low-fat dough as the base for two types of individual pizzas and for focaccia. The basic dough can be prepared a day in advance and stored in an airtight plastic bag in the refrigerator.

Individual Shrimp and Pesto Pizzas

1 prepared recipe Pizza Dough
(page 101)

1 tablespoon cornmeal

1 cup fresh basil leaves

1 teaspoon chopped garlic

2 tablespoons freshly squeezed
lemon juice

1 tablespoon water

4 ounces peeled, deveined, and cooked
shrimp, roughly chopped

2 ounces red onion, thinly sliced

2 teaspoons freshly grated
Parmesan cheese

Preheat the oven to 450 degrees.

Cut the dough into 8 equal pieces and work each into a 4-inch circle. Scatter the cornmeal on a large nonstick baking sheet and place the dough circles on top. Bake for about 5 minutes, just until they begin to color. Remove from the oven, leaving the oven on.

While the dough is baking, combine the basil and garlic in the bowl of a food processor. Turn the machine on and process for about 1 minute, while drizzling in the lemon juice and water through the feed tube, to form a paste.

Spread 2 teaspoons of the basil paste on each pizza. Scatter the shrimp and onion evenly over the basil. Top each with 1/4 teaspoon of the Parmesan cheese.

Bake the pizzas for 7 to 8 minutes, until golden.

YIELD—EIGHT 4-INCH PIZZAS

Fat per pizza—0.80 g.

Calories per pizza—203.5

Individual Scallop and Cilantro Pizzas

½ cup water

¼ cup dry white wine

4 ounces sea scallops, each cut in half horizontally to form 2 thin circles

1 prepared recipe Pizza Dough (page 101)

1 tablespoon cornmeal

1⅓ cups fresh cilantro leaves, lightly packed

1 teaspoon chopped garlic

2 tablespoons lemon juice

3 tablespoons Vegetable Stock (page 7)

½ cup thinly sliced roasted bell pepper (see Pantry)

In a small saucepan, bring the water and white wine to a boil over high heat. Cover, reduce the heat to medium-low, and simmer for 5 minutes. Add the scallops and poach for 3 minutes. Remove from the heat and drain the liquid from the pan.

Preheat the oven to 450 degrees.

Cut the dough into 8 equal pieces and work each into a 4-inch circle. Place on a large nonstick baking sheet that has been dusted with the cornmeal. Bake the dough for about 5 minutes, until colored slightly, and remove it from the oven.

Meanwhile, combine the cilantro and garlic in a food processor. With the machine on, drizzle in the lemon juice and vegetable stock, processing just until a paste forms.

Spread 1 tablespoon of the cilantro paste on each pizza. Divide the scallops among the pizzas and scatter the roasted pepper strips on top.

Bake the pizzas for 7 to 8 minutes, until golden.

YIELD—EIGHT 4-INCH PIZZAS

Fat per pizza—0.66 g.

Calories per pizza—203.5

Sun-Dried Tomato, Red Onion, and Black Olive Focaccia

8 sun-dried tomatoes

1/2 cup boiling water

1 prepared recipe Pizza Dough (page 101)

1 teaspoon cornmeal

1 teaspoon minced garlic

3 ounces red onion, thinly sliced

3 large black Mission or manzanilla olives, finely chopped

1 tablespoon chopped fresh basil

Combine the tomatoes and boiling water in a small bowl and set aside for 30 minutes to reconstitute.

Transfer half the pizza dough to a work surface. Punch down and flatten it into a 7-inch circle. Place on a pizza paddle or a portable cutting board dusted with the cornmeal if you will be using a baking stone; otherwise, place it on a large inverted baking sheet dusted with cornmeal. Cover loosely with plastic wrap and set aside for about 1 1/2 hours to rise again.

Preheat the oven to 500 degrees; if using a baking stone, preheat the stone.

Remove the tomatoes from the soaking liquid and thinly slice.

Flatten and spread the dough into a 10-inch circle. Prick all over with the tines of a fork. Scatter the garlic evenly over the dough. Scatter subsequent layers of tomato, onion, olives, and basil. Lightly press the toppings down into the dough.

Transfer to the preheated baking stone or put into the oven on the inverted baking sheet. Place 2 ice cubes directly on the bottom shelf of the oven. Bake for about 17 minutes, until the focaccia is golden and the edges sound hollow when tapped.

Cool on a wire rack.

Desserts

Cakes

AND

Cookies

Banana Bread Cake

½ cup natural unsweetened applesauce

¼ cup nonfat sour cream

1 cup granulated sugar

1 cup dark brown sugar (not packed)

¾ cup nonfat liquid egg substitute

1½ cups mashed banana (3–4 soft medium-size bananas)

1 teaspoon baking soda

3 cups all-purpose flour

2 teaspoons baking powder

½ teaspoon salt

½ cup buttermilk

1 teaspoon vanilla extract

Light vegetable oil cooking spray

1 prepared recipe Marshmallow Meringue Frosting (page 194)

Preheat the oven to 350 degrees.

Put the applesauce, sour cream, and sugars in a bowl and combine with an electric mixer set at medium speed. Add the liquid egg substitute ¼ cup at a time, combining thoroughly after each addition. Beat in the banana and baking soda.

Combine the flour, baking powder, and salt in a sifter. Sift about half into the applesauce mixture. Fold in ¼ cup of the buttermilk. Sift in the remaining flour mixture and fold in the remaining buttermilk. Stir in the vanilla.

Spray two 8-inch round cake pans lightly with vegetable oil spray and spread the oil to coat the surface of each. Divide the batter between the pans. Bake for about 30 minutes, until the sides begin to pull away from the pans and a tester inserted into the cakes comes out clean.

Remove the pans to wire racks and allow the cakes to cool completely. Cut each cake in half horizontally to form 4 layers. Frost between layers and the outside of the cake with the marshmallow meringue frosting.

YIELD—14 SERVINGS

Fat per serving (including frosting)—0.46 g.

Calories per serving (including frosting)—285.0

We've concocted a comfort dessert that's reminiscent of the banana bread Mom used to send you at college—turned into a layer cake and dressed up for company in a fluffy meringue frosting.

It's a bit of an indulgence from the calorie perspective, but then we all need a lot of comfort these days. For a slimmed down variation, skip the frosting, cut each layer into 14 servings, and dust with confectioners' sugar.

Cocoa Decadence with Raspberry Sauce

1 cup cake flour

1¼ cups unsweetened Dutch-processed cocoa powder

⅓ cup natural unsweetened applesauce

1⅓ cups granulated sugar

8 large eggs, whites only (do not combine), at room temperature

¾ cup buttermilk

1½ teaspoons vanilla extract

Light vegetable oil cooking spray

Up to 1 teaspoon confectioners' sugar

1 prepared recipe Raspberry Sauce (page 190)

½ pint fresh raspberries for garnish (optional)

Preheat the oven to 350 degrees.

Sift the flour and cocoa together and set aside.

Combine the applesauce and granulated sugar in a large mixing bowl and beat with an electric mixer set at medium-high until blended. Turn the mixer to low and add the whites of 2 eggs, the buttermilk, and the vanilla. Continue to beat until the ingredients are well combined. Stir in the flour mixture until the batter is blended. Set aside.

Using a clean bowl and clean beaters, beat the whites of the remaining 6 eggs at medium-high until stiff peaks are formed. Add a third of the beaten egg white to the batter and stir until fully incorporated. Gently fold in the remaining egg white.

Spray a 9-inch springform pan once lightly with the vegetable oil spray and smooth the oil evenly over the surface. Pour the batter into the pan. Bake for 20 to 25 minutes, just until the cake is beginning to become firm in the center and to pull away from the sides of the pan.

Transfer the pan to a wire rack and allow to cool for at least 2 hours.

Remove the springform and dust the cake with confectioners' sugar (sprinkle the sugar through a small sieve for even dusting). Cut the cake into serving pieces and spoon 1 tablespoon of the raspberry sauce over each portion. Garnish with raspberries, if desired.

YIELD—16 SERVINGS

Fat per serving (including sauce)—0.90 g.
Calories per serving (including sauce)—130.6

Classic Cheesecake

CRUST:

1/4 cup nonfat cream cheese

1/2 cup confectioners' sugar, sifted

1/4 cup nonfat liquid egg substitute

1 teaspoon vanilla extract

1/2 teaspoon grated lemon zest

1 cup plus 2 tablespoons all-purpose flour, sifted

Pinch of salt

Light vegetable oil cooking spray

FILLING:

2 cups nonfat vanilla Yogurt Cheese (see Pantry)

1 1/4 cups nonfat ricotta cheese

1 1/2 cups granulated sugar

1 1/4 cups nonfat liquid egg substitute

2 tablespoons all-purpose flour

1 teaspoon lemon zest

2 teaspoons vanilla extract

1/3 cup evaporated skim milk

Preheat the oven to 350 degrees.

To make the crust, combine the cream cheese, sifted confectioners' sugar, and liquid egg substitute in a mixing bowl. Beat with an electric mixer set at medium speed (if using a stationary electric mixer, fit it with the paddle attachment) just until the sugar is incorporated, about 30 seconds. Don't be concerned if the cream cheese is not fully dissolved.

Add the vanilla, lemon zest, sifted flour, and salt. Beat at low speed for about 15 seconds, until you have a crumbly dough mixture that has not yet formed into a ball.

Spray a 9-inch springform pan once lightly with the vegetable oil spray and spread the oil over the surface. Transfer the dough to the springform. With lightly floured hands, press it down evenly to cover the bottom.

Bake in the center of the oven for 10 to 12 minutes, until golden brown. Remove to a wire rack to cool, turn the oven down to 325 degrees, and place a baking pan three quarters filled with water on the bottom rack.

For the filling, combine the yogurt and ricotta cheeses and beat with an electric mixer set at medium speed until smooth. Beat in the granulated sugar until well blended. Add the liquid egg substitute $\frac{1}{4}$ cup at a time, beating after each addition until well incorporated. Beat in the flour, lemon zest, vanilla, and evaporated skim milk at low speed.

Pour the batter over the crust, set the springform pan on a cookie sheet, and position it on the center rack over the pan of water. Bake for 1 hour and 20 minutes to 1 hour and 25 minutes, until golden and firm in the center.

Cool in the pan on a wire rack for at least 2 hours. Cover and refrigerate for at least 4 hours more before serving.

YIELD—12 SERVINGS

Fat per serving—0.29 g.
Calories per serving—219.6

Cappuccino Angel Food Cake

1 1/2 cups sugar

3 1/2 tablespoons unsweetened Dutch-processed cocoa powder

3 tablespoons boiling water

1 1/4 teaspoons vanilla extract

1 cup sifted cake flour

1/4 teaspoon salt

2 teaspoons ground cinnamon

12 large eggs, whites only, at room temperature

1 1/4 teaspoons cream of tartar

Preheat the oven to 350 degrees.

Put the sugar into the bowl of a food processor and process for 2 minutes.

Combine the cocoa powder, boiling water, vanilla, and 1/2 cup of the sugar in a small bowl. Whisk until smooth and glossy.

Mix the flour, salt, and cinnamon together in a small bowl and set aside.

In a large bowl, beat the egg whites until frothy. Add the cream of tartar and continue to beat until soft peaks form. Slowly add the remaining cup of sugar. Beat until stiff peaks form. Whisk about 1 cup into the chocolate mixture.

Quickly fold the flour mixture into the egg whites, 1/4 cup at a time. When completely incorporated, fold in the chocolate and pour the batter into a 10-inch tube pan. Bake for about 40 minutes, until a tester inserted into the cake comes out clean.

Gently turn the cake upside down and suspend it, so that air can circulate beneath, by placing a wine bottle or another cone-shaped object up through the tube. (The cake must cool upside down, or it will deflate. Don't worry that the cake will fall while suspended, as it will adhere tightly to the inside of the pan.) Let cool for about 1½ hours. Run a spatula around the outer edge to loosen before removing the cake from the pan.

YIELD—16 SERVINGS

Fat per serving—0.19 g.
Calories per serving—115.0

Chewy Chocolate Sour Cherry Cookies

1 cup all-purpose flour

$^3/_4$ teaspoon baking powder

$^1/_2$ teaspoon baking soda

$^1/_2$ teaspoon salt

$^1/_2$ cup unsweetened Dutch-processed cocoa powder

1$^1/_2$ cups instant rolled oats

$^1/_2$ cup natural unsweetened applesauce

$^1/_4$ cup mashed banana

$^1/_2$ cup light brown sugar, firmly packed

$^1/_4$ cup light corn syrup

1 large egg, white only, beaten

1 teaspoon vanilla extract

$^3/_4$ cup dried sour cherries

Preheat the oven to 350 degrees.

Combine the flour, baking powder, baking soda, salt, cocoa powder, and rolled oats in the bowl of a food processor. Process for about 1 minute, until well blended. Set aside.

Mix the applesauce, banana, brown sugar, and corn syrup together in a large bowl. Stir in the beaten egg white, then the vanilla. Add the oat mixture, blend well, and fold in the sour cherries.

Using 1$^1/_2$ to 2 tablespoons of dough for each cookie, drop onto ungreased cookie sheets about 2 inches apart. Bake for about 15 minutes, until firm to the touch.

Cool the cookies on a wire rack.

YIELD—ABOUT 30 COOKIES

Fat per cookie—0.47 g.

Calories per cookie—71.7

Individual
Strawberry Shortcakes

FILLING:

1 pint strawberries, hulled and
   quartered

1/4 cup sugar

2 tablespoons Grand Marnier liqueur

TOPPING:

1/2 cup evaporated skim milk,
   well chilled

1 tablespoon Grand Marnier liqueur

SHORTCAKES:

1 prepared and baked recipe
   Buttermilk Biscuits (page 10)

Put a metal mixing bowl and the beaters for an electric mixer into the freezer to chill.

For the filling, combine the strawberries, sugar, and the Grand Marnier in a bowl. Mix and set aside.

For the topping, put the evaporated skim milk into the chilled mixing bowl. Fit the electric mixer with the chilled beaters and beat at medium speed until soft peaks form. Add the liqueur and continue to mix for 1 minute more.

To assemble, split each buttermilk biscuit in half and place one half on each dessert plate. Divide the strawberries among the biscuits. Place the other half of each biscuit, slightly askew, on top of the strawberries, leaving a mound of fruit exposed, and top each with a dollop of the whipped evaporated milk.

YIELD—8 SERVINGS

Fat per serving—0.97 g.
Calories per serving—208.7

What could possibly be more festive than strawberry shortcake? Mounds of orange liqueur—marinated berries on a delicate biscuit with a silky topping.

Muesli Cookies

1³/₄ cups nonfat muesli with raisins

1¹/₂ cups all-purpose flour

1 teaspoon baking soda

³/₄ teaspoon baking powder

¹/₂ teaspoon salt

¹/₂ teaspoon ground cinnamon

³/₄ cup natural unsweetened applesauce

²/₃ cup dark brown sugar, firmly packed

3 tablespoons dark corn syrup

1 large egg, white only, well beaten

1 teaspoon vanilla extract

Preheat the oven to 375 degrees.

Combine the muesli, flour, baking soda, baking powder, salt, and cinnamon in a bowl and mix thoroughly.

In a second, larger bowl, combine the applesauce, brown sugar, and corn syrup. Stir in the egg white, vanilla, and then the muesli mixture. Combine well.

Drop about 2 tablespoons of dough at a time onto ungreased cookie sheets, leaving 2 inches of space between each cookie. Bake for about 14 minutes, until dark brown.

Remove the cookies to a wire rack to cool.

YIELD—ABOUT 25 COOKIES

Fat per cookie—0.13 g.

Calories per cookie—79.1

Sugarless Cranberry-Apple Cookies

¹/₂ cup all-purpose flour

1 cup whole wheat flour

1 cup wheat germ

³/₄ cup rolled oats

1 tablespoon baking powder

2 teaspoons ground cinnamon

One 12-ounce can unsweetened frozen apple juice concentrate, thawed

¹/₃ cup natural unsweetened applesauce

2 large eggs, whites only

1 cup dried cranberries

Light vegetable oil cooking spray

Preheat the oven to 375 degrees.

In a large mixing bowl, whisk together the dry ingredients.

Combine the apple juice concentrate, applesauce, egg whites, and cranberries in a blender. Blend at low speed just until the cranberries are coarsely chopped. Add the mixture to the dry ingredients and stir to combine thoroughly.

Spray 2 cookie sheets lightly with the vegetable oil spray and distribute the oil evenly. Drop the batter by the half tablespoonful onto the cookie sheets. Bake for 8 to 10 minutes, until the cookies are a light golden brown.

Transfer the cookie sheets to a wire rack and cool for a minute or two. Remove the cookies to a plastic storage bag; this will keep them moist. When the cookies have cooled completely, seal the bag to preserve freshness.

YIELD—ABOUT 60 COOKIES

Fat per cookie—0.34 g.

Calories per cookie—35.4

Lots of spice and everything nice, but there's no sugar in these little treats. Since they're a healthy snack for kids and an almost guiltless indulgence for their elders, we make a big batch.

This is real old-time chocolate cake—the kind you take a big chunk of to bed with a glass of milk. And there's almost no fat, since we replace the usual butter with buttermilk and applesauce and the typical melted chocolate with cocoa powder. The light, crumbly texture comes from beating in each egg white individually.

Old-Fashioned Chocolate Cake with Chocolate Frosting

1 3/4 cups all-purpose flour

1/2 cup unsweetened Dutch-processed
    cocoa powder, plus 1 1/2 teaspoons
    for dusting

1 teaspoon baking soda

1/2 teaspoon salt

1/2 cup natural unsweetened applesauce

3 tablespoons light corn syrup

1 cup sugar

3 large eggs, whites only, at room
    temperature

1 cup buttermilk

Light vegetable oil cooking spray

1 prepared recipe Chocolate Frosting
    (page 192)

Preheat the oven to 350 degrees.

Sift the flour, 1/2 cup of cocoa powder, baking soda, and salt together into a medium-size bowl. Set aside.

In a large bowl, combine the applesauce and corn syrup. Beat with an electric mixer set at medium speed until blended. While continuing to beat, gradually add the sugar. While beating at high speed, add the egg whites, one at a time. Continue to beat until the mixture is light and frothy.

Reduce the speed to medium and beat in half of the flour mixture, then 1/2 cup of the buttermilk, until incorporated. Beat in the rest of the flour, then the remaining 1/2 cup of buttermilk. With a rubber spatula, scrape down the sides of the bowl.

Spray two 8-inch round, nonstick cake pans lightly with the vegetable oil spray and spread the oil evenly. Dust each with 3/4 teaspoon of the remaining cocoa powder. Divide the batter between the cake pans. Bake for 25 to 30 minutes, until a toothpick inserted into the center of each cake comes out clean.

Transfer the pans to a wire rack and cool for 15 minutes, then remove the cakes from the pans to cool completely.

When the cakes have cooled, frost with the chocolate frosting. Let sit for 1 hour before serving.

YIELD—12 SERVINGS

Fat per serving (including frosting)—0.88 g.
Calories per serving (including frosting)—230.2

Poppy Seed Cake with Lemon Glaze

1 cup sifted cake flour

2 tablespoons poppy seeds

1 teaspoon baking powder

¼ teaspoon salt

5 canned apricot halves

1 cup sugar

¼ cup water

2 teaspoons vanilla extract

5 large eggs, whites only, at room temperature

Light vegetable oil cooking spray

1 prepared recipe Lemon Glaze (page 195)

Preheat the oven to 350 degrees.

In a bowl, stir together the flour, poppy seeds, baking powder, and salt until well combined. Set aside.

Puree the apricot halves to a smooth consistency in a food processor or blender. (You should have about 3 rounded tablespoons.)

Transfer the apricot puree to a large mixing bowl. While beating with an electric mixer set at medium-high, gradually add ¾ cup of the sugar, producing a thick, pale mixture that resembles beaten egg yolk. Turn the mixer to low and add the water and vanilla. Gradually add the flour mixture, continuing to beat until incorporated into the batter.

Using a clean bowl and clean beaters, beat the egg whites at medium-high until thick. Gradually add the remaining ¼ cup of sugar, beating until stiff peaks form and the meringue mixture looks glossy. Stir a third of the meringue into the batter to lighten it, then fold in the remainder.

Spray the interior of a 10-inch bundt pan once lightly with the vegetable oil spray and spread the oil to coat. Pour the batter into the prepared bundt pan. Bake until a tester comes out clean and the center of the cake springs back to the touch, about 25 minutes.

Transfer to a wire rack and cool in the pan for 30 to 40 minutes. Remove the cooled cake from the pan, place on the rack set over a pan to catch the drippings, and spoon lemon glaze over the cake.

YIELD—12 SERVINGS

Fat per serving (including glaze)—0.57 g.
Calories per serving (including glaze)—157.3

Carrot Cake

1 pound carrots, peeled

1½ cups seedless raisins

1½ cups whole wheat flour

1 cup all-purpose flour

1 tablespoon ground cinnamon

2 tablespoons baking powder

One 12-ounce can unsweetened frozen apple juice concentrate, thawed

2 tablespoons dark corn syrup

1 tablespoon vanilla extract

4 large eggs, whites only, at room temperature

1¼ cups natural unsweetened applesauce

1 prepared recipe Creamy Yogurt Cheese Frosting (page 191)

Preheat the oven to 350 degrees.

Cut circles of baker's parchment to line the bottoms of two 9-inch cake pans.

Grate the carrots into a bowl (you should have about 2½ cups grated carrots). Mix in the raisins and set aside.

In a large mixing bowl, combine the flours, cinnamon, and baking powder. Add the apple juice concentrate, corn syrup, and vanilla. Combine with an electric mixer set at medium speed. Beat in the egg whites, one at a time, mixing well after each addition, and the applesauce. Stir in the carrot and raisin mixture.

Pour the batter into the lined cake pans. Bake for 40 to 45 minutes, until a tester inserted into the cakes comes out clean.

Remove the cakes from the pans and cool on wire racks. Peel the parchment from the bottom of the cooled cakes. Frost with yogurt cheese frosting. Once frosted, the cake must be stored in the refrigerator.

YIELD—12 SERVINGS

Fat per serving (including frosting)—0.43 g.

Calories per serving (including frosting)—242.4

Flourless Chocolate Fruit Cake

1/2 cup seedless raisins

1/2 cup golden raisins

1/3 cup chopped pitted dates

1/3 cup dried strawberries

1/3 cup dried cranberries

1/2 cup cream sherry

5 large eggs, whites only

2 tablespoons natural unsweetened applesauce

1 1/4 cups Grape-Nuts cereal, finely ground

1 cup sugar

1/3 cup nonfat liquid egg substitute

1/4 cup unsweetened Dutch-processed cocoa powder

1 1/2 tablespoons light corn syrup

1/2 teaspoon ground cloves

1 tablespoon freshly squeezed lemon juice

1 1/2 teaspoons baking powder

1/4 cup apricot spreadable fruit

Confectioners' sugar for dusting

A heavenly creation that's not exactly a chocolate cake and far from a traditional fruitcake (no candied fruit in sight), but incorporates elements of both.

Preheat the oven to 350 degrees.

Cut baker's parchment to fit the bottom of 2 nonstick 8-inch cake pans.

Combine the raisins, dates, strawberries, cranberries, and sherry in a bowl and set aside.

Beat the egg whites to soft peaks and set aside.

In a large bowl, combine the applesauce, Grape-Nuts, and sugar, blending thoroughly. Whisk in the liquid egg substitute in 2 batches. Add the cocoa powder, corn syrup, cloves, lemon juice, and baking powder; mix well. Mix in the reserved raisin mixture. Fold in the egg whites.

Pour the batter into the lined pans and bake for about 30 minutes, until the edges begin to pull away from the sides of the pan and a tester inserted into the cakes comes out clean.

Transfer the pans to wire racks and let cool for about 15 minutes. Remove the cakes from the pans and allow to cool completely. Peel the parchment from the cakes. Smooth on the fruit spread between the layers and dust the top with a little powdered sugar sifted through a small sieve.

YIELD—14 SERVINGS

Fat per serving—0.31 g.

Calories per serving—209.1

Fudgy Raspberry Brownies

3/4 cup unsweetened Dutch-processed cocoa powder

1/4 cup light corn syrup

1 cup natural unsweetened applesauce

1/2 teaspoon salt

1 teaspoon vanilla extract

2 cups sugar

2 large eggs, whites only, at room temperature

1/2 cup nonfat liquid egg substitute

1/2 cup all-purpose flour

3/4 cup seedless raspberry spreadable fruit

Cut baker's parchment to fit the bottom of an 8- × 8-inch nonstick cake pan.

Combine the cocoa powder, corn syrup, and applesauce in a large bowl. Whisk until smooth and glossy. Mix in the salt, vanilla, and sugar.

Using an electric mixer set at low speed, sequentially beat in 1 egg white, 1/4 cup of the liquid egg substitute, the remaining egg white, and the remaining 1/4 cup of egg substitute, mixing well after each addition. Beat in the flour.

Pour half the batter (about 2 cups) into the pan. Freeze for 1 hour until solid.

Smooth the fruit spread on top and pour the rest of the batter over the fruit. Allow the frozen batter to reach room temperature, about 40 minutes.

Meanwhile, preheat the oven to 325 degrees.

Bake the brownies for 40 to 45 minutes, until just set (they will no longer wiggle in the center when the pan is shaken) and a tester comes out slightly sticky.

Cool on a wire rack for 1 to 2 hours, then chill for at least 2 hours. Cut into 2- × 1-inch pieces.

YIELD—32 BROWNIES

Fat per brownie—0.23 g.

Calories per brownie—90.2

Tarts, Pies,
AND
Pastries

Pear Tart

2 Bartlett pears (about 12 ounces), cored and quartered

3 tablespoons pear nectar

3 tablespoons ginger eau-de-vie or Poire William

1/2 tablespoon freshly squeezed lemon juice

1/2 cup nonfat liquid egg substitute

1/4 cup sugar

1/2 cup skim milk

1 teaspoon arrowroot dissolved in 1 tablespoon water

1/3 cup plain nonfat yogurt

1 prepared and baked Phyllo Crust (page 139)

Cut each pear into 16 thin slices and put into a bowl. Add 2 tablespoons of the pear nectar, 1 tablespoon of the liqueur, and the lemon juice. Mix and set aside to soak.

Combine the liquid egg substitute, 3 tablespoons of the sugar, and the milk in the top of a double boiler over boiling water. Cook for about 3 minutes over high heat, whisking constantly until the sugar dissolves.

Remove the top of the double boiler from the heat and whisk in the remaining pear nectar and liqueur, along with the arrowroot mixture. Fold in the yogurt. Cover and chill for at least 1 hour, or until ready to assemble the tart.

Preheat the oven to 375 degrees.

Spread the chilled custard evenly over the bottom of the phyllo crust. Drain the pear slices and arrange them in a spiral with the thick ends toward the center, mounding a few slices in the middle. Sprinkle with 1/2 tablespoon of the sugar. Bake for 15 minutes.

Remove the pie from the oven and turn on the broiler. Sprinkle the remaining 1/2 tablespoon of sugar over the pie. Position about 6 inches from the heat source and broil for about 1 1/2 minutes, just long enough to caramelize the sugar.

Remove to a wire rack, cool to room temperature, and serve immediately.

YIELD—8 SERVINGS

Fat per serving—0.60 g.

Calories per serving—147.9

Pear slices are suspended in a delicate, foamy custard in this lovely tart. For macerating the fruit and flavoring the custard, we like the accent lent by a ginger brandy, but pear brandy works equally well and carries out the main theme of the tart.

Sweet Potato Pie

This pie has a character quite distinct from pumpkin, its uptown counterpart—less sweet and encompassing a much more complex medley of flavors.

Bake the piecrust just before starting this recipe, so that it will have cooled for only about 10 minutes when you turn in the filling.

¹/₄ cup seedless raisins

¹/₄ cup brandy

1 pound sweet potatoes (about 2 potatoes)

2 large eggs, whites only

1 tablespoon buttermilk

¹/₄ cup light brown sugar (not packed)

3 tablespoons nonfat liquid egg substitute

¹/₄ cup evaporated skim milk

¹/₂ teaspoon ground cinnamon

¹/₈ teaspoon grated nutmeg

1 prepared and baked Nutty Crust (page 140)

Preheat the oven to 350 degrees.

Combine the raisins and brandy in a small bowl and set aside to soak.

Microwave the sweet potatoes at full power for about 7 minutes, until soft, or bake them in a 350 degree oven for about 45 minutes, until fork tender.

Meanwhile, beat the egg whites to stiff peaks.

Cut the cooked potatoes in half and scoop the flesh from the skin into a large mixing bowl. Add the buttermilk and mash with a fork, leaving some chunks intact. Add the brown sugar and mix a bit to break it up. Add the liquid egg substitute, the evaporated skim milk, and the spices, mixing thoroughly. Mix in the raisins and brandy.

Fold the beaten egg white into the mixture and turn into the crust. Bake for about 40 minutes, until a tester comes out clean.

Remove to a wire rack and allow to cool.

YIELD—10 SERVINGS

Fat per serving—0.49 g.
Calories per serving—115.1

Chocolate-Dipped Cannoli

Light vegetable oil cooking spray

12 square won ton wrappers

2 tablespoons granulated sugar

FILLING:

2 cups nonfat ricotta cheese

1 cup confectioners' sugar

1/2 cup finely minced dried apricot

1/4 cup finely minced candied ginger

1 teaspoon vanilla extract

CHOCOLATE DIP:

2 tablespoons confectioners' sugar, sifted

1 tablespoon unsweetened Dutch-processed cocoa powder, sifted

2 teaspoons apricot brandy or light rum

Preheat the oven to 375 degrees.

Bring a pot of water to a boil and fill a large bowl with ice water. Spray 4 cannoli forms very lightly with the vegetable oil spray, rubbing the oil evenly over the surface.

Prepare the won ton wrappers in batches of 4. Boil the wrappers for 2 minutes, immediately submerge them in the ice water, remove, and pat dry. Roll each won ton around a cannoli form, starting with a corner. Place on a nonstick baking sheet. Bake for 15 minutes.

Remove the pan from the oven, roll each cannoli in granulated sugar, and bake for 10 minutes more. Remove from the oven, allow to cool for 5 minutes, and twist the cannoli off the forms. Repeat the process until all 12 cannoli are cooked.

For the filling, combine all the ingredients in a bowl, and mix thoroughly. Fill each cannoli with about 1/4 cup of the mixture, pushing the filling down into the shell.

For the chocolate dip, combine all the ingredients in a small bowl. Whisk until smooth and glossy. Spread 1/2 teaspoon on each end of each cannoli.

YIELD—12 SERVINGS

Fat per serving—0.41 g.

Calories per serving—133.7

We make this favorite Italian delicacy healthier and easier with a little transcultural wizardry —baking nonfat won ton wrappers for shells instead of making and deep-frying pastry dough.

The cannoli forms are readily available in packages of 4 from kitchenware stores. Both the shells and the filling can be prepared a day in advance (store the shells in an airtight container and the filling in the refrigerator), but once assembled the cannoli must be refrigerated and are best used within the same day.

Chocolate Mousse Pie

This is our update of the traditional chocolate chiffon pie, made healthy (no raw egg white and almost no fat) and given a bit of a continental flair with the addition of liqueur to flavor the chocolate.

1½ cups skim milk

1 packet unflavored gelatin

⅔ cup sugar

¼ cup nonfat liquid egg substitute

½ cup unsweetened Dutch-processed cocoa powder

1 tablespoon Grand Marnier, Triple Sec, or other orange-flavored liqueur

½ cup evaporated skim milk, well chilled

1 prepared and baked Phyllo Crust (page 139)

Put a metal mixing bowl and the beaters for an electric mixer into the freezer to chill.

Pour the skim milk into a saucepan. Sprinkle the gelatin on top and allow about 3 minutes for the mixture to set. Add the sugar and egg substitute, whisking until thoroughly blended. Cook over medium heat for about 6 minutes, stirring constantly, until thick enough to coat the back of a spoon.

Whisk in the cocoa powder and liqueur, whisking until completely dissolved. Transfer to a bowl, cover, and refrigerate for 15 minutes.

Put the evaporated milk into the chilled metal bowl. Fit the electric mixer with the chilled beaters and beat at high speed until stiff peaks form. Mix in the chocolate mixture and pour into the phyllo crust. Cover and chill for 2 to 3 hours before serving.

YIELD—10 SERVINGS

Fat per serving—0.82 g.

Calories per serving—135.6

Banana Cream Pie

¾ cup sugar

¼ cup cornstarch

⅛ teaspoon salt

2¼ cups skim milk

¼ cup nonfat liquid egg substitute

1¼ teaspoons vanilla extract

1 prepared and baked Nutty Crust
(page 140)

1½ large bananas (about 12 ounces),
cut into ¼-inch slices
(about 1½ cups)

Combine the sugar, cornstarch, and salt in a saucepan. Slowly whisk in the milk. Whisk in the liquid egg substitute. Bring to a boil over medium-high heat, stirring constantly. Reduce the heat to low and cook, stirring, for 2 minutes more.

Remove the pan from the heat and stir in the vanilla. Pour half (about 1¼ cups) into the crust. Set aside for about 15 minutes to cool.

Layer the bananas onto the partially filled shell and spread the remaining filling on top. Cover and chill until set, about 1 hour.

YIELD—8 SERVINGS

Fat per serving—0.68 g.

Calories per serving—180.9

A traditional treat in a trim new outfit, with no cream in sight. We like to add a bit of sophistication to this long-time diner fare by serving each slice with a dollop of Crème Fraîche (page 185) on top.

Lime Meringue Pie

A little bit like lemon meringue, its common cousin, this beautifully peaked pie has a personality all its own.

1 1/2 cups plus 6 tablespoons sugar

5 tablespoons cornstarch

1 tablespoon all-purpose flour

1/8 teaspoon salt

1/2 cup freshly squeezed, strained lime juice (about 4 limes)

1/2 cup cold water, plus 1 1/3 cups boiling water

1/4 cup nonfat liquid egg substitute

1 prepared and baked Phyllo Crust (page 139)

3 large eggs, whites only

1 teaspoon cream of tartar

Preheat the oven to 350 degrees.

Combine 1 1/2 cups of the sugar, the cornstarch, flour, and salt in a saucepan. Whisking constantly, slowly add the lime juice. Whisk in the cold water and continue whisking until thoroughly blended and smooth. Whisk in the liquid egg substitute. Slowly whisk in the boiling water. Bring the mixture to a boil over medium-high heat, stirring constantly. Reduce the heat to medium-low and cook, stirring constantly, for 1 minute.

Pour into the phyllo crust and set aside.

Put the egg whites into a mixing bowl and beat by hand or with an electric mixer set at medium speed until they're frothy and beginning to form soft peaks. Add the cream of tartar and continue beating until stiff peaks begin to form. Beat in the remaining 6 tablespoons of sugar, a tablespoon at a time. Beat until stiff, but still glossy, peaks form. Spread the meringue over the top of the pie, swirling it into peaks.

Bake for about 15 minutes, until the peaks of the meringue have browned.

Cool on a wire rack, then chill for about 1 hour before serving.

YIELD—10 SERVINGS

Fat per serving—0.29 g.

Calories per serving—223.1

No-Bake Orange Cheese Pie

1/2 cup freshly squeezed orange juice

1 packet unflavored gelatin

1 cup nonfat vanilla Yogurt Cheese
(see Pantry)

1/2 cup sugar

1/2 cup skim milk

1 cup low-fat (1%) cottage cheese

1 prepared and baked Nutty Crust
(page 140)

2 teaspoons grated orange zest

Put the orange juice in a small saucepan, sprinkle the gelatin on top, and allow about 3 minutes to set. Warm over low heat, stirring constantly, just until the gelatin is dissolved and the mixture begins to steam. Remove the pan from the heat and set aside.

Combine the yogurt cheese and sugar in a bowl and beat with an electric mixer set at medium speed until well blended. Beat in the gelatin mixture, a little at a time, mixing until well incorporated after each addition. Beat in 1/4 cup of the skim milk. Cover and chill for about 15 minutes, until slightly thickened.

Combine the remaining 1/4 cup of skim milk and the cottage cheese in a blender and mix at high speed until smooth. Fold into the chilled yogurt cheese mixture and pour into the crust. Cover and refrigerate for 45 minutes.

Garnish with the orange zest before serving.

YIELD—8 SERVINGS

Fat per serving—0.78 g.
Calories per serving—131.8

Pumpkin Mincemeat Pie

1 cup pumpkin puree

1/2 cup dark brown sugar, firmly packed

1 teaspoon ground cinnamon

1/2 teaspoon ground allspice

1/2 teaspoon grated nutmeg

1/4 teaspoon salt

1/2 cup nonfat liquid egg substitute

3/4 cup evaporated skim milk

1 1/4 cups mincemeat

1 prepared and baked Phyllo Crust (page 139)

Preheat the oven to 450 degrees.

Combine the pumpkin, brown sugar, cinnamon, allspice, nutmeg, salt, liquid egg substitute, and evaporated milk in a large mixing bowl. Using an electric mixer set at medium speed, beat until the mixture is smooth and thick, about 1 minute. (You can also whisk, allowing a bit more time.)

Spread the mincemeat evenly over the bottom of the phyllo crust. Pour the pumpkin mixture on top. Bake for 10 minutes. Lower the oven temperature to 350 degrees, and bake for 40 to 45 minutes more, until the pie is firm in the center.

Transfer to a wire rack and let cool to room temperature. Serve immediately or chill before serving, as desired.

YIELD—10 SERVINGS

Fat per serving—0.65 g.

Calories per serving—169.2

Crêpes Suzette

1 cup sifted all-purpose flour

1/2 cup nonfat liquid egg substitute

2 large eggs, whites only

1/4 teaspoon salt

3/4 cup skim milk

1/2 cup orange marmalade

2 tablespoons Grand Marnier liqueur

2 teaspoons confectioners' sugar
(optional)

Combine the flour, liquid egg substitute, egg whites, salt, and skim milk in a mixing bowl and whisk to a smooth, pourable batter. Set aside for 5 minutes.

Make the crêpes in a preheated nonstick crêpe pan, a 6-inch nonstick frying pan, or an electric crêpe maker. Use about 3 tablespoons of the batter for each, or just enough to coat the surface. Cook just on one side for about 1 minute, over medium heat if on the stove top, until the edges are firm and the crêpe is lightly browned. Remove from the pan and roll up.

Meanwhile, combine the marmalade and liqueur in a small saucepan. Warm over medium-low heat for 2 to 3 minutes, until steaming.

Serve 3 crêpes on each plate, topped with about 2 1/2 tablespoons of the sauce. Dust with confectioners' sugar, if desired.

YIELD—4 SERVINGS

Fat per serving—0.33 g.

Calories per serving—261.4

We've done away with the fat and stop short of the flambé, but this old standby remains a favorite. It's always great fun to prepare, especially if you have a crêpe maker.

Fresh Strawberry Tart

1 cup skim milk

¹/₂ cup nonfat liquid egg substitute

3 tablespoons sugar

1 tablespoon freshly squeezed orange juice

1 prepared and baked Phyllo Crust (page 139)

2 pints strawberries, washed and hulled

¹/₃ cup red currant jelly

Warm the milk in a small saucepan over low heat just until it begins to give off steam. Remove from the heat.

Combine the egg substitute and sugar in a mixing bowl, whisking to combine thoroughly. While continuing to whisk, slowly pour in the warm milk. Return the mixture to the saucepan over low heat. Cook for 3 to 4 minutes, stirring constantly, until barely thickened, just enough to lightly coat the back of a spoon. Pour into a bowl. Stir in the orange juice.

Spread the custard evenly over the phyllo crust. Place the strawberries, hulled side down, into the custard.

Put the jelly into a small, microwave-safe bowl and microwave at full power until melted, about 1 minute. (You can also melt the jelly by warming it in a small saucepan over low heat for 2 to 3 minutes.) Spoon evenly over the strawberries.

Serve immediately or chill until ready to serve.

YIELD—8 SERVINGS

Fat per serving—0.70 g.

Calories per serving—161.5

Phyllo Crust

Light vegetable oil cooking spray
6 sheets phyllo dough

About ½ cup pear nectar
4 teaspoons sugar

Preheat the oven to 400 degrees.

Spray a 9-inch oven-proof glass pie plate lightly with the vegetable oil spray and distribute the oil evenly over the surface.

Remove 6 sheets of phyllo dough from the package, lay them out on a work surface, and cover with a moist towel during assembly.

Remove the first sheet and lay it across the plate, draping an even amount over each side. Paint with pear nectar and sprinkle with ½ teaspoon of sugar. Lay the second sheet on top going in the opposite direction, paint with nectar, and sprinkle with ½ teaspoon of sugar. Layer 3 more sheets going in alternating directions and painting and sprinkling with sugar between the layers. Lay the last sheet on top and sprinkle with sugar, but do not paint.

Moisten your fingers with pear nectar. Starting at one of the corners between the longer overlaps of dough, gather up the dough, fold it in, and crimp it down along the lip of the pie plate. Working quickly, continue the process all the way around the plate. Paint the crust with nectar and sprinkle with the remaining 1 teaspoon of sugar. Bake for about 10 minutes, until light gold and crisp.

Remove to a wire rack and let cool completely, about 30 minutes.

YIELD—ONE 9-INCH PIECRUST

Light and flaky phyllo dough makes a wonderful crust— low in fat and easy to execute—that we use as the shell for a number of our pies. The only trick to working with phyllo is not to let it dry out. Keep the sheets covered with a damp towel until you are ready to use them and proceed without any lengthy interruption once you start the assembly. You can prepare and bake the crust a day before making a pie, wrap it in aluminum foil, and store it at room temperature.

In this basic recipe, we call for painting the phyllo with pear nectar, but other fruit nectars may be substituted, such as strawberry nectar when preparing a phyllo crust for the Fresh Strawberry Tart (preceding recipe).

This almost effortless piecrust, which we use for several recipes, has an almond taste with none of the fat. The secret? Grape-Nuts Flakes, which provide the nutty taste, just as Grape-Nuts provided texture and flavor to the Flourless Chocolate Cake in our original 99% Fat-Free Cookbook.

Nutty Crust

2 cups Grape-Nuts Flakes cereal

2 teaspoons ground cinnamon

1 large egg, white only

2 tablespoons freshly squeezed orange juice

Light vegetable oil cooking spray

Preheat the oven to 350 degrees.

Put the cereal into the bowl of a food processor and process to fine crumbs, about 2 minutes.

Transfer to a bowl and mix in the cinnamon. Add the egg white and orange juice. Mix thoroughly.

Spray an 8-inch pie plate once lightly with the vegetable oil spray and spread the oil evenly to coat. Turn the cereal mixture into the plate. Press down with moistened fingers to form a shell. Bake for 10 minutes.

Remove to a wire rack and cool for about 15 minutes.

YIELD—ONE 8-INCH PIECRUST

Fruit Desserts

Peaches Poached in Champagne Served with Strawberry Sauce

2 cups dry champagne

1 1/2 cups water

1 cinnamon stick

3 leaves fresh basil

2 whole cloves

6 large, firm peaches (about 2 pounds), peeled, halved, and stoned

1 prepared recipe Strawberry Sauce (page 189)

Combine the champagne, water, cinnamon, basil, and cloves in a large, straight-sided frying pan. Bring to a boil over medium heat. Boil for 1 minute and reduce the heat to low. Add the peaches, stoned side down, and simmer for about 10 minutes, until just fork tender.

Remove the pan from the heat and allow the peaches to cool in the liquid for about 20 minutes.

Transfer the contents of the pan to a bowl, cover, and chill for at least 2 to 3 hours.

For each portion, serve 2 peach halves, topped with about 3 table-spoons of strawberry sauce.

YIELD—6 SERVINGS

Fat per serving (including sauce)—0.25 g.

Calories per serving (including sauce)—70.8

Not only can this dessert be made a day in advance, but the longer the peaches chill in their aromatic poaching liquid— redolent of cinnamon and clove and imparting a hint of licorice from the basil—the better they taste.

Strawberries and Kiwifruit in Ginger Crème

3/4 cup Crème Fraîche (page 185)

2 teaspoons finely chopped fresh ginger

1 pint strawberries, washed and hulled

2 kiwis (about 7 ounces), peeled

Combine the crème fraîche and ginger in a bowl and set aside for 15 minutes.

Quarter the strawberries. Cut each kiwi into 8 spears and each spear into thirds. Put the fruit into a bowl and toss to mix.

Serve 1/2 cup of the fruit mixture in each of 6 champagne boats, topping with 2 tablespoons of the ginger crème.

YIELD—6 SERVINGS

Fat per serving (including crème)—0.37 g.

Calories per serving (including crème)—49.5

Apple Cobbler

Light vegetable oil cooking spray

2 cups peeled and sliced McIntosh apples (about 2 apples)

8 cups peeled and sliced Jonathan apples (about 8 large apples)

1 1/4 cups sugar

1/4 cup all-purpose flour

1/4 teaspoon grated nutmeg

1/2 teaspoon ground cinnamon

1/8 teaspoon ground cloves

1/2 tablespoon freshly squeezed lemon juice

1 recipe Buttermilk Biscuits (page 10), prepared up to rolling out the dough

Preheat the oven to 375 degrees.

Spray a 13- × 9- × 1 1/2-inch baking dish once lightly with the vegetable oil spray and spread the oil evenly over the surface.

Combine the apples, sugar, flour, spices, and lemon juice in a large bowl. Mix thoroughly and transfer the mixture to the baking dish.

On a lightly floured work surface, roll out and shape the biscuit dough into a 13- × 9-inch rectangle. Place over the baking dish, crimping the dough to the edges. Cut 6 to 8 slits across the top with a sharp knife. Bake for 35 to 40 minutes, until the crust is brown and the filling is bubbly.

YIELD—12 SERVINGS

Fat per serving—0.89 g.

Calories per serving—237.7

This makes a nice change of pace from the more common peach cobbler. It's good by itself, but if a topping is desired, add 2 tablespoons honey and 2 teaspoons lemon zest to our Crème Fraîche (page 185).

Glazed Pears in Crispy Cups

Light vegetable oil cooking spray

6 round won ton wrappers

3/4 cup orange juice

1/3 cup plus 1/2 tablespoon granulated sugar

1/2 cup orange marmalade

4 Bartlett pears (about 1 1/2 pounds), peeled, cored, and sliced lengthwise

1 teaspoon grated lemon zest

2 tablespoons freshly squeezed lemon juice

1/2 tablespoon confectioners' sugar

Preheat the oven to 375 degrees.

Put a pot of water up to boil and fill a large bowl with ice water.

Turn a nonstick muffin tin upside down and spray the outside lightly with the vegetable oil spray to cover 6 of the inverted wells. Spread the oil evenly to coat the wells.

Cook the won ton wrappers in the boiling water for 2 minutes, remove and submerge quickly in the ice water, and pat dry. Drape each wrapper over a prepared well of the inverted tin. Paint the won ton circles with a little of the orange juice and sprinkle 1/4 teaspoon of the granulated sugar over each. Bake for 18 to 20 minutes, until golden. Remove from the oven and set aside.

Combine 1/2 cup of the orange juice, 1/3 cup of the sugar, and the orange marmalade in a large frying pan. Bring to a boil over medium heat. Reduce the heat to low and simmer for about 3 minutes, until the mixture has thickened. Stir in the pears, lemon zest, and lemon juice.

Cover and cook for about 10 minutes more, until the pears are fork tender. Uncover and cook for an additional 4 minutes, until the pears have browned lightly. Stir, remove from the heat, and cool for 10 minutes.

Remove the pastry cups from the muffin tin and place a cup on each of 6 dessert plates. Divide the glazed pears among the cups. Dust each with a little confectioners' sugar.

YIELD—6 SERVINGS

Fat per serving—0.66 g.
Calories per serving—221.4

Gratin of Fresh Fig

A simple low-fat custard holds this dish together without distracting from the delightful flavor of fresh figs. Using a wide, shallow gratin dish—or individual oven-proof glass casseroles—allows for even browning of the entire top surface.

Light vegetable oil cooking spray

8 ounces fresh purple figs (about 8 figs), sliced into 1/4-inch rounds

1/2 cup evaporated skim milk

1/4 cup nonfat liquid egg substitute

2 tablespoons honey

1 tablespoon cognac

1/2 teaspoon freshly grated nutmeg

1 tablespoon all-purpose flour

Preheat the broiler.

Spray 1 large or 4 individual gratin dishes lightly with the vegetable oil spray. Cover the bottom of the gratin dish(es) with a single layer of fig rounds.

Combine the remaining ingredients in a mixing bowl. Whisk until the flour is completely dissolved. Pour over the figs. Broil for 3 to 4 minutes, until bubbly and lightly browned. Serve immediately.

YIELD—4 SERVINGS

Fat per serving—0.48 g.

Calories per serving—118.5

Raspberries Romanoff

¹/₄ cup nonfat liquid egg substitute

¹/₃ cup sugar

¹/₃ cup cream sherry

¹/₃ cup Crème Fraîche (page 185)

1 ¹/₃ cups evaporated skim milk,
    well chilled

1 pint fresh raspberries

Put a metal mixing bowl and the beaters for an electric mixer into the freezer to chill.

Combine the liquid egg substitute and sugar in the top of a double boiler over boiling water. Cook for about 1 minute over medium heat, stirring constantly, until foamy. Add the cream sherry. Continue to cook and stir until the mixture is thick enough to coat the back of a spoon, about 4 minutes. Pour into a bowl, cover, and refrigerate for 20 minutes.

When chilled, add the crème fraîche and whisk to blend.

Using the chilled mixing bowl and beaters, beat the evaporated milk with an electric mixer set at medium speed until stiff peaks form. Fold into the custard mixture.

Layer each of 6 balloon wineglasses with ¹/₄ cup of custard and 2 ounces of the raspberries. Top each with a little of the remaining custard.

YIELD—6 SERVINGS

Fat per serving—0.44 g.

Calories per serving—141.7

We replace the traditional strawberries with raspberries and the whipped cream with our own low-fat Crème Fraîche, but this resounding finale lives up to its heritage.

Caramel Baked Apples on Puff Pastry

4 square won ton wrappers

3 tablespoons orange juice

2 teaspoons granulated sugar

1 teaspoon confectioners' sugar

4 Royal Gala or other firm, sweet
    apples (about 1 pound), peeled,
    cored, and cut into 8 wedges each

2 tablespoons dark brown sugar

2 tablespoons brandy

$1/4$ cup Crème Fraîche
    (optional, page 185)

Preheat the oven to 375 degrees.

Put a pot of water up to boil and fill a large bowl with ice water.

Cook the won ton wrappers in the boiling water for 2 minutes, remove and submerge quickly in the ice water, and pat dry. Place on a nonstick baking sheet. Bake for 10 minutes.

Remove from the oven, paint the won ton squares with a little orange juice, sprinkle each with $1/2$ teaspoon of the granulated sugar, and bake for about 8 minutes more, until golden. Remove the baking sheet from the oven and turn on the broiler. Dust each square with $1/4$ teaspoon of confectioners' sugar.

Place the apple wedges in a single layer on a microwave-safe glass pie plate. Combine the brown sugar and brandy in a small bowl, mixing until the sugar is thoroughly dissolved. Pour over the apples and toss to coat. Microwave at full power for $1 1/2$ minutes, rotate 180 degrees, and cook for about $1 1/2$ minutes more, until fork tender. (The apples can also be baked in a 375 degree oven for 10 minutes.)

Spoon the sauce back over the apples and broil (4 to 6 inches from the heat source) for about 3 minutes, until lightly browned.

Spoon the apples and sauce onto the baked squares and top each, if desired, with 1 tablespoon of crème fraîche.

YIELD—4 SERVINGS

Fat per serving—0.41 g.
Calories per serving—142.2

Peach Brown Betty

4 slices French Bread (page 9)

$^2/_3$ cup light brown sugar (not packed)

$^1/_2$ teaspoon ground cinnamon

$^1/_4$ teaspoon grated nutmeg

Light vegetable oil cooking spray

2 pounds peaches (about 6 large peaches), peeled, stoned, and sliced (about 3 cups)

2 tablespoons freshly squeezed lemon juice

$^1/_4$ cup water

Toast the French bread on both sides in the broiler, taking care not to burn it. Remove the toast and turn the oven down to 400 degrees to preheat.

Coarsely chop the toast into tiny cubes (not as fine as crumbs). You should have about 1 cup. Set aside.

Combine the brown sugar, cinnamon, and nutmeg in a small bowl and mix thoroughly.

Spray an 11- × 7$^1/_2$- × 2-inch baking dish once lightly with vegetable oil spray and spread the oil evenly over the surface.

Put $^1/_3$ cup of the toast cubes on the bottom of the dish. Layer half of the peaches on top and sprinkle $^1/_3$ cup of the brown sugar over the peaches. Layer another $^1/_3$ cup of toast cubes, the rest of the peaches, and the remaining $^1/_3$ cup of brown sugar. Top with the remaining $^1/_3$ cup of toast cubes.

Pour the lemon juice and water over the top layer. Cover securely with aluminum foil and bake for 30 minutes. Remove the foil and bake for about 10 minutes more, until brown.

YIELD—6 SERVINGS

Fat per serving—0.30 g.
Calories per serving—127.7

Bananas Flambé

4 very ripe bananas, unpeeled

2 tablespoons apricot nectar

3 tablespoons chopped dried apricots

1/4 cup orange marmalade

1/4 cup water

1/2 cup brandy

1 matchbook from a fairly pretentious restaurant

Preheat the oven to 350 degrees.

Trim both ends from each banana, leaving the peels intact. Place on a cookie sheet lined with aluminum foil and bake for about 15 minutes, until the skins have turned black. Set aside to cool.

Combine the apricot nectar, dried apricots, orange marmalade, and water in a nonstick frying pan. Cook over medium heat just until the mixture begins to bubble (do not bring to a boil). Remove from the heat.

Peel the bananas, roll each in the sauce to coat, and plate individually.

Warm the brandy over medium heat just until it begins to give off steam. Transfer to a chafing dish to keep warm.

When ready to serve, ignite the brandy and gently pour a little over each banana.

YIELD—4 SERVINGS

Fat per serving—0.60 g.

Calories per serving—254.8

The days when head waiters flamboyantly ignited dishes at tableside may be fleeting childhood memories, but who says we can't put on a show for old time's sake?

Frozen Desserts

Apple Pie Ice Cream

1 large McIntosh apple (about 10
ounces)

1 small Granny Smith apple
(about 6 ounces)

¹/₄ teaspoon freshly squeezed
lemon juice

¹/₄ cup water

¹/₄ cup dark brown sugar, firmly packed

¹/₂ teaspoon ground cinnamon

1 cup buttermilk

1 tablespoon Cuarenta y Tres liqueur

Peel and core the apples. Cut each into 12 slices, then cut each slice in half crosswise. Combine in a saucepan with the lemon juice and water. Cook for 15 minutes over medium heat, stirring occasionally.

Remove the pan from the heat and mash the apples coarsely with a potato masher. Transfer about three quarters of the contents of the pan to the bowl of a food processor or blender and puree. Return to the pan and stir in the brown sugar and cinnamon. Allow the mixture to cool to room temperature, transfer it to a bowl, cover, and refrigerate for 45 minutes to 1 hour.

Stir in the buttermilk and liqueur.

Process in an ice cream maker according to the manufacturer's instructions.

YIELD—ABOUT 1 PINT (4 SERVINGS)

Fat per serving—0.79 g.

Calories per serving—143.3

No need for pie à la mode when you serve this creamy frozen buttermilk treat, which has luscious baked apple in it already.

We're partial to Cuarenta y Tres, a vanilla liqueur, but you can easily use cognac instead.

What better finale could there be for Thanksgiving dinner? The intense, rich flavor of this seasonal delight can be enjoyed all year round if you load the freezer up with cranberries during the holidays. For a festive summertime presentation, serve the sorbet in hollowed-out orange cups.

The addition of vodka keeps this silky sorbet from freezing into a harder granita texture.

Cranberry-Orange Vodka Sorbet

1¹/₃ cups sugar

1¹/₃ cups water

2 cups whole cranberries
(about 10 ounces)

¹/₄ cup plus 2 tablespoons
freshly squeezed orange juice

2 tablespoons vodka

Combine the sugar, water, and cranberries in a saucepan. Bring to a boil over high heat. (The cranberries will pop as the water boils.) Reduce the heat to medium and cook for an additional 4 minutes.

Puree the mixture in a blender. Transfer to a bowl, stir in the orange juice and vodka, cover, and chill in the freezer for about 2 hours.

YIELD—ABOUT 1¹/₂ PINTS (6 SERVINGS)

Fat per serving—0.12 g.

Calories per serving—204.3

Persimmon Frozen Yogurt

1/4 cup Triple Sec liqueur

1 packet unflavored gelatin

1/3 cup water

1/3 cup sugar

One 10-ounce very ripe Japanese persimmon, peeled and cubed

3/4 cup plain nonfat yogurt, chilled

Put the liqueur into a small bowl, sprinkle the gelatin on top, and allow about 2 minutes for the mixture to set.

Combine the water and sugar in a small saucepan. Bring to a boil over medium-high heat, stirring constantly until the sugar dissolves. Boil for 5 minutes. Remove from the heat and stir in the gelatin mixture. Return the pan to the heat just until the contents begin to smoke, about 1 minute. Cover and chill for 30 minutes.

Puree the persimmon in a food processor or blender.

Put the yogurt into a bowl and stir in the chilled syrup. Add the persimmon puree and blend thoroughly.

Process in an ice cream maker according to the manufacturer's instructions.

YIELD—ABOUT 1 PINT (4 SERVINGS)

Fat per serving—0.15 g.

Calories per serving—166.9

Be sure to use a very ripe persimmon, which, like most of us, mellows with age. Underripe persimmons can pack quite a pucker. Grand Marnier or any other orange-flavored liqueur may be substituted for the Triple Sec.

Espresso Granita

1 1/2 cups freshly brewed hot espresso

1/4 cup plus 2 tablespoons sugar

4 thin slices lemon rind (optional)

Combine the espresso and sugar in a bowl, stirring until the sugar is completely dissolved. Cover and freeze for 3 hours.

Chop the granita into rough crystals before serving. Garnish each serving, if desired, with a thin slice of lemon rind.

YIELD—ABOUT 1 PINT (4 SERVINGS)

Fat per serving—0 g.

Calories per serving—74.2

Mango-Champagne Sorbet

¹/₂ cup dry champagne   1 can (about 11¹/₂ ounces) mango nectar

Combine the ingredients and process in an ice cream maker according to the manufacturer's instructions.

YIELD—ABOUT 1 PINT (4 SERVINGS)

Fat per serving—0.05 g.

Calories per serving—76.3

We serve this ethereal and excruciatingly easy sorbet as an antidote to spicy entrées. It also works well as a palate cleanser between courses.

Chocolate Sorbet

¹/₂ cup sugar

¹/₄ cup plus 2 tablespoons unsweetened
   Dutch-processed cocoa powder

³/₄ cup boiling water

2 teaspoons vanilla extract

Combine the sugar and cocoa powder in a small saucepan. Add the boiling water and stir until completely dissolved. Bring to a boil over medium heat and boil for 3 minutes. Cover and chill for 30 minutes.

Stir in the vanilla.

Process in an ice cream maker according to the manufacturer's instructions.

YIELD—ABOUT 1 PINT (4 SERVINGS)

Fat per serving—0.84 g.

Calories per serving—111.6

Peach Frozen Yogurt

¹/₃ cup sugar

¹/₃ cup water

4 large very ripe peaches (about 1¹/₂
    pounds), peeled, stoned, and cut
    into chunks

1 cup plain nonfat yogurt, chilled

Combine the sugar and water in a small saucepan. Bring to a boil over medium heat, stirring until the sugar is dissolved. Boil for 5 minutes, remove from the heat, and cool to room temperature.

Meanwhile, puree the peaches to a smooth consistency in a food processor or blender.

Put the yogurt into a mixing bowl. While whisking, drizzle in the cooled syrup. Add the peach puree and whisk until well blended.

Process in an ice cream maker according to the manufacturer's instructions.

YIELD—ABOUT 1 PINT (4 SERVINGS)

Fat per serving—0.16 g.

Calories per serving—145.9

A bit creamier than a sorbet, but still light and fruity.

Pear-Port Sorbet

½ cup port wine   1 can (about 11½ ounces) pear nectar

Combine the port and nectar in a bowl or a large measuring cup. Cover and chill in the freezer for 10 minutes.

Process in an ice cream maker according to the manufacturer's instructions.

YIELD—ABOUT 1 PINT (4 SERVINGS)

Fat per serving—0.08 g.

Calories per serving—97.5

Tequila-Lime Sorbet

3/4 cup sugar

1 1/4 cups water

1/2 cup freshly squeezed lime juice

1 teaspoon grated lime zest

1 tablespoon tequila

Bring the sugar and water to a boil in a small saucepan. Reduce the heat to low and cook for 5 minutes more.

Remove the pan from the heat and allow the syrup to cool to room temperature. Add the lime juice, lime zest, and tequila. Cover and chill for 30 minutes.

Process in an ice cream maker according to the manufacturer's instructions.

YIELD—ABOUT 1 PINT (4 SERVINGS)

Fat per serving—0.05 g.

Calories per serving—156.5

Crisp, tart, and packing a bit of a kick!

Banana-Rum Granita

¹/₂ cup light rum   1 can (about 11 ¹/₂ ounces) banana nectar

Combine the rum and nectar in a bowl, cover, and freeze for 3 hours.
Chop the granita into rough crystals and divide into 4 portions.

YIELD—ABOUT 1 PINT (4 SERVINGS)

Fat per serving—0.1 g.
Calories per serving—120.0

White Wine-Strawberry Sorbet

$^1/_2$ cup dry white wine

1 can (about 11$^1/_2$ ounces) strawberry
   nectar

4 whole strawberries (optional)

Combine the wine and the nectar in a bowl or a large measuring cup, cover, and refrigerate for 30 minutes.

Process in an ice cream maker according to the manufacturer's instructions.

Transfer the sorbet to 4 balloon wineglasses and top each serving, if desired, with a strawberry.

YIELD—ABOUT 1 PINT (4 SERVINGS)

Fat per serving—0.08 g.

Calories per serving—75.0

The delectably light combination of dry wine and natural fruit nectar is not to be confused with the heavier sensation of fruit-flavored wine. Use this recipe as a base for experimentation with any of the variety of refreshing nectars now on the market.

Toffee Crunch Frozen Yogurt

$1/3$ cup plus $1/2$ cup sugar	1 cup plain nonfat yogurt
$1/3$ cup plus 1 tablespoon water	$2/3$ cup buttermilk
Light vegetable oil cooking spray	

Combine $1/3$ cup of the sugar and $1/3$ cup of the water in a small saucepan. Bring to a boil over medium-high heat, stirring until the sugar dissolves. Boil for 5 minutes. Cover and refrigerate the syrup for 30 minutes.

Spray a nonstick baking sheet once lightly with the vegetable oil spray and spread the oil evenly over the surface. Set aside.

Combine the remaining $1/2$ cup of sugar and 1 tablespoon of water in a saucepan. Stir to blend. Cook over medium heat for about 10 minutes, stirring constantly until the mixture caramelizes and turns brown. Turn onto the prepared baking sheet and tilt the sheet back and forth to distribute evenly. Allow to cool completely, about 10 minutes.

Peel the hardened toffee from the sheet in chunks and break it into small pieces, reserving 4 larger chunks for garnish. Transfer the small pieces to a food processor and process to powder. Keep $1/4$ cup of the powder out. Seal the remainder in an airtight container and refrigerate.

Remove the chilled syrup from the refrigerator and fold in the yogurt. Stir in the buttermilk.

Process in an ice cream maker according to the manufacturer's instructions. When the mixture is half frozen, stir in the $1/4$ cup of toffee powder evenly.

Divide the frozen yogurt into 4 servings. Sprinkle some of the remaining toffee powder over each and garnish with a chunk of toffee.

YIELD—ABOUT 1 PINT (4 SERVINGS)

Fat per serving—0.44 g.

Calories per serving—201.4

Soufflés, Puddings, AND Mousses

Mocha Mousse

1 tablespoon instant coffee granules

1 tablespoon unsweetened Dutch-
   processed cocoa powder

1/4 cup Kahlúa liqueur

2 large eggs, whites only

1 packet unflavored gelatin

1/2 cup sugar

1 cup evaporated skim milk

A truly distinctive dessert—light in texture, but with a rich, complex flavor. Try it with Crème Anglaise (page 186).

Place a metal mixing bowl and the beaters for an electric mixer into the freezer to chill.

Combine the instant coffee granules, cocoa powder, and liqueur in a small bowl, stirring until the coffee and cocoa are completely dissolved. Set aside.

Put the egg whites in the top of a double boiler and sprinkle the gelatin over them. Allow 3 to 4 minutes for the mixture to set.

Meanwhile, put water up to boil in the bottom of the double boiler.

Fit the top onto the double boiler over the boiling water. Whisk in the coffee mixture. Cook over medium-low heat for about 3 minutes, stirring constantly, until the mixture has thickened. Remove the pan from the heat and the top from the bottom of the double boiler. Whisk in the sugar, continuing to whisk for 1 to 2 minutes, until the sugar is completely dissolved and the mixture has cooled. Set aside for a few minutes more to cool to room temperature and thicken.

Using the chilled mixing bowl and beaters, beat the evaporated milk at high speed until soft peaks form. Beat in the cooled egg white mixture until thoroughly combined. Transfer to a serving bowl, cover, and chill for at least 30 minutes before serving.

YIELD—6 SERVINGS

Fat per serving—0.19 g.

Calories per serving—132.8

Apricot Soufflé with Apricot Sauce

8 ounces dried apricots

³/₄ cup plus 2 tablespoons sugar

1 ¹/₂ cups plus 1 tablespoon water

Light vegetable oil cooking spray

¹/₂ tablespoon all-purpose flour

1 tablespoon Triple Sec liqueur

4 large eggs, whites only, at room temperature

Confectioners' sugar for dusting

Combine the apricots, ³/₄ cup of the sugar, and 1 ¹/₂ cups of the water in a small saucepan. Bring to a boil over medium heat, reduce the heat to low, cover, and simmer for 20 minutes.

After the mixture has simmered for about 10 minutes, preheat the oven to 375 degrees. Spray a 1-quart soufflé dish or straight-sided casserole once lightly with the vegetable oil cooking spray and smooth the oil evenly over the surface. Dust with a tablespoon of the remaining sugar.

Transfer the apricot mixture to a food processor or blender and puree. (You should have about 1 ¹/₂ cups apricot puree.)

Return half of the puree to the pan. Mix in the remaining tablespoon of water and the flour. Cook over low heat, stirring constantly, just until the mixture begins to give off steam. Remove the pan from the heat and mix in the Triple Sec. Set aside.

Whisking by hand or using a heavy stationary mixer set at medium-low speed, beat the egg whites to soft peaks. Add the remaining tablespoon of sugar and continue to beat until stiff, moist peaks are formed.

Transfer the apricot and flour mixture to a large mixing bowl. Fold in a third of the egg whites until thoroughly incorporated. Gently fold in the remaining egg whites. Pour into the prepared soufflé dish or casserole. With your finger, make a ¹/₂- to ³/₄-inch deep ridge around the inside rim of the dish. Bake for 15 to 18 minutes, until the top of the soufflé has puffed up and browned.

Meanwhile, heat the remaining apricot puree in a small saucepan to make a sauce.

Dust the soufflé with confectioners' sugar. Scoop the soufflé out of its dish with a large spoon, as you would pudding, drizzle with sauce, and serve immediately.

YIELD—4 SERVINGS

Fat per serving (including sauce)—0.11 g.
Calories per serving (including sauce)—301.6

This decadent, velvety dessert derives its special character from nutty basmati rice and an infusion of rich cocoa custard. We borrowed the original recipe from our friend and fellow cookbook author Jill Van Cleave and pared the fat and calories by substituting a cocoa powder and corn syrup mixture for chunk chocolate and evaporated skim milk for half-and-half.

To pull out all the stops, top each serving with a dollop of Crème Fraîche (page 185).

Jill's Basmati Rice Pudding with Cocoa Custard

FUDGE CUSTARD:

3/4 cup unsweetened Dutch-processed cocoa powder

1/4 cup light corn syrup

1 1/4 cups evaporated skim milk

1/3 cup sugar

1/2 cup nonfat liquid egg substitute, lightly beaten

1/2 teaspoon vanilla extract

RICE PUDDING:

1/2 cup basmati rice

1 cup skim milk

1 1/4 cups evaporated skim milk

1/4 cup sugar

1/2 teaspoon vanilla extract

Light vegetable oil cooking spray

About 6 cups boiling water

For the custard, combine the cocoa powder and corn syrup in a bowl and mix thoroughly.

Warm the evaporated milk and sugar in a small saucepan, stirring to dissolve the sugar, just until the milk begins to give off steam. Immediately pour over the cocoa mixture and stir until smooth. Stir in the liquid egg substitute and vanilla. Set aside.

For the pudding, combine the rice and skim milk in the top of a double boiler over simmering water. Cover and cook over medium-low heat for about 45 minutes, until most of the liquid has been absorbed and the rice is tender but not soft.

Remove the pan from the heat and stir in the evaporated milk, sugar, and vanilla. Add the reserved cocoa custard and stir until well mixed.

Preheat the oven to 350 degrees.

Spray a 2-quart baking dish with the vegetable oil spray and spread the oil over the surface. Add the pudding. Place the baking dish into a deep baking pan large enough for the dish to sit flat on the bottom. Fill the pan with boiling water halfway up the sides of the baking dish.

Bake for 50 minutes to 1 hour, until the pudding has just set (it should shiver when the dish is shaken gently). Remove the pudding from the water bath to a wire rack. Cool to room temperature, about 30 minutes.

Serve immediately in shallow bowls; do not chill.

YIELD—10 SERVINGS

Fat per serving—0.92 g.
Calories per serving—184.6

Crème Brûlée

3 cups evaporated skim milk

1 cup nonfat liquid egg substitute

1/2 cup plus 2 tablespoons sugar

1 teaspoon vanilla extract

Preheat the oven to 350 degrees.

Combine the evaporated milk and 1/4 cup of the sugar in a heavy-bottomed medium-size saucepan over medium heat, stirring to blend. Scald until bubbles begin to form around the outside edge and the milk begins to steam, about 5 minutes.

Put the liquid egg substitute into a bowl. While whisking, slowly add the scalded milk. Return the mixture to the saucepan. Cook for about 4 minutes over medium heat, stirring constantly until thick enough to coat the back of a spoon. Remove the pan from the heat and mix in the vanilla.

Transfer 3/4 cup of the custard to each of six 8-ounce ramekins and set them into a baking dish. Fill the dish with hot tap water up to the level of the custard. Bake for about 40 minutes, until the custard is set in the center and a tester comes out clean.

Remove the ramekins to a wire rack and cool for about 15 minutes. Then cover each individually and chill for at least 2 hours.

Preheat the broiler.

Unwrap the ramekins and sprinkle 1 tablespoon of the remaining sugar over each. Position the ramekins close to the heat source and broil for 1 to 1 1/2 minutes, until browned, taking care not to burn the sugar.

Chill for at least 1 hour more, and serve within 4 hours.

YIELD—6 SERVINGS

Fat per serving—0.3 g.
Calories per serving—198.3

Raspberry Mousse

¼ cup light rum

1 packet unflavored gelatin

10 ounces frozen raspberries

1 cup evaporated skim milk

3 tablespoons confectioners' sugar

Place a metal mixing bowl and the beaters for an electric mixer in the freezer to chill.

Put the rum into a small bowl, sprinkle the gelatin on top, and let sit for about 2 minutes to gel.

Puree the raspberries in a blender or food processor. Transfer to a small saucepan and stir in the gelatin. Warm for about 1 minute over medium heat, stirring constantly, until a light foam appears on the surface. Remove from the heat and set aside to cool completely.

Pour the evaporated milk into the chilled mixing bowl. Using the chilled beaters, beat at high speed until the beaters begin to leave a trail of ribbons across the surface. Add the confectioners' sugar and continue to beat until stiff peaks form. Beat in the cooled raspberry mixture.

Cover and refrigerate for 1 hour before serving.

YIELD—6 SERVINGS

Fat per serving—0.18 g.

Calories per serving—123.1

Refreshing and fruity, this mousse by itself is the perfect ending to a rich meal. We also like it with Cappuccino Angel Food Cake (page 114) or atop a bowl of fresh raspberries.

Russian Cream

1/4 cup cold water, plus 3/4 cup boiling water

1 packet unflavored gelatin

1/2 cup sugar

1 cup evaporated skim milk

1 cup low-fat (1%) cottage cheese

1/2 tablespoon vanilla extract

1 pint fresh strawberries, washed, hulled, and quartered

Put the cold water into a mixing bowl, sprinkle the gelatin on top, and allow to sit for 2 minutes. Add the sugar and boiling water, stirring until the sugar is completely dissolved. Stir in 1/2 cup of the evaporated milk. Cover and refrigerate for 20 minutes to thicken.

Combine the remaining 1/2 cup of evaporated milk, the cottage cheese, and the vanilla in a blender. Blend at high speed until smooth. Whisk into the chilled mixture, continuing to whisk until bubbly.

Pour into a 1-quart ring mold, cover, and chill for at least 3 hours, until firm. (The cream may be chilled overnight.)

Unmold onto a serving plate and mound the strawberries in the center.

YIELD—6 SERVINGS

Fat per serving—0.63 g.
Calories per serving—150.3

Fig Mousse with Fig Sauce

1 pound dried Calimyrna figs, stemmed (about 18)

1 cup water, plus ¼ cup warm water

¼ cup sugar

1 packet unflavored gelatin

1 teaspoon plus up to another 2 tablespoons crème de cassis

¾ cup evaporated skim milk, well chilled

Place a metal mixing bowl and the beaters from an electric mixer into the freezer until well chilled.

Put the figs and ¾ cup of the water in a saucepan. Bring to a boil over high heat. Cover, reduce the heat to medium-low, and simmer for about 10 minutes, until the figs are plump and soft. Transfer to a food processor or blender and puree.

Combine the sugar and gelatin in a small saucepan. Stir in the remaining ¼ cup of water. Let sit for 1 minute, then cook for about 3 minutes over low heat, stirring constantly, until completely dissolved.

Transfer to a bowl. Add 1 cup of the fig puree, 1 teaspoon of the crème de cassis, and the ¼ cup of warm water. Cover and refrigerate for 1 hour.

In the chilled bowl using the chilled beaters, beat the evaporated skim milk at high speed just until stiff. Stir about ¼ of the whipped evaporated milk into the chilled fig and cassis mixture, then return that combination to the chilled mixing bowl and beat at high speed.

For the sauce, combine the remaining ¾ cup of fig puree with up to 2 tablespoons of crème de cassis, as desired.

Serve the mousse in 4-ounce ramekins or parfait glasses, drizzled with sauce.

YIELD—8 SERVINGS

Fat per serving (including sauce)—0.36 g.

Calories per serving (including sauce)—106.9

An intense dessert that combines the distinctive taste of figs with a fruity hint of currant, topped by a dense sauce of similar composition. If you prefer a thinner sauce, add up to 2 tablespoons boiling water.

Individual Pear Soufflés

4 ounces dried pears

1/3 cup plus 2 tablespoons sugar

3/4 cup plus 1 tablespoon water

Light vegetable oil cooking spray

1 tablespoon cornstarch

1 tablespoon ginger or pear brandy

5 large eggs, whites only, at room temperature

Preheat the oven to 375 degrees.

Combine the dried pears, 1/3 cup of the sugar, and 3/4 cup of the water in a microwave-safe container. Cook in a microwave oven at full power, uncovered, for about 5 minutes, until the fruit is fork tender. To cook on the stove top, bring the mixture to a boil in a small saucepan over medium heat. Cover, reduce the heat to low, and simmer for 20 to 25 minutes, until the pears are very soft.

Meanwhile, spray 4 individual 1-cup soufflé dishes very lightly with vegetable oil spray and spread the oil evenly. Dust each with 3/4 teaspoon of the sugar.

Puree the pear mixture in a food processor or blender. (You should have about 3/4 cup of puree; if not, stir in boiling water to reach that volume.)

Remove the puree to a small saucepan. Add the cornstarch and the remaining tablespoon of water. Cook over low heat, stirring constantly, just until the mixture begins to steam. Remove from the heat and stir in the brandy.

Whisk the egg whites to soft peaks, or beat in a heavy stationary mixer set at medium-low speed. Mix in the remaining tablespoon of sugar. Continue to whisk or beat until stiff, moist peaks form.

Transfer the pear mixture to a large bowl. Fold in a third of the egg whites until thoroughly incorporated. Gently fold in the remaining egg whites. Divide the mixture among the 4 prepared dishes. Run your finger around the inside rim of each dish to make a small ridge.

Bake for 15 to 18 minutes, until the soufflés have puffed up and browned. Serve immediately.

YIELD—4 SERVINGS

Fat per serving—0.43 g.
Calories per serving—198.8

Rum-Raisin Bread Pudding

1/3 cup light rum

1/2 cup seedless raisins

3 cups evaporated skim milk

1 cup nonfat liquid egg substitute

2/3 cup light brown sugar, firmly packed

1 1/2 teaspoons vanilla extract

5 ounces (about 1/3 loaf) French bread (page 9), cut into 1-inch cubes

Combine the rum and raisins in a small bowl and set aside for 15 minutes.

In a large bowl, whisk together the evaporated milk, liquid egg substitute, brown sugar, and vanilla. Stir in the raisins, rum, and the bread cubes and set aside for 20 minutes.

Preheat the oven to 350 degrees.

Bring a kettle of water to a boil.

Pour the pudding mixture into a 9 1/4-inch nonstick loaf pan. Place the pan in the center of a baking pan or large oven-proof casserole and position it in the middle of the oven. Pour boiling water into the pan to reach halfway up the sides of the loaf pan. Bake until the pudding is set in the center, 45 to 55 minutes.

Remove the loaf pan to a wire rack to cool. Chill before serving. Turn the pudding onto a serving plate and slice.

YIELD—10 SERVINGS

Fat per serving—0.26 g.

Calories per serving—212.5

Toppings, Sauces, AND Frostings

Crème Fraîche

1 cup plain nonfat Yogurt Cheese   2 tablespoons buttermilk
   (see Pantry)

Combine the yogurt cheese and buttermilk in a mixing bowl and stir gently to blend. Cover with plastic wrap and set aside at room temperature for 18 hours.

Chill for 1 to 2 hours before serving. The crème fraîche will keep for up to a week in the refrigerator.

YIELD—ABOUT 1 CUP

Fat per tablespoon—0.03 g.
Calories per tablespoon—7.3

Buttermilk culture thickens the yogurt cheese in this healthy rendition, much as unpasteurized cream thickens the whipping cream in the original French version. In addition to the numerous uses we suggest in our recipes, this crème adds a special touch to almost any fruit or plain cake. For an interesting taste twist, add 1 tablespoon unsweetened cocoa powder before chilling the crème fraîche.

This custardy vanilla sauce so resembles the classic French topping that we've borrowed the name. Try it drizzled on the Mocha Mousse (page 171), the Individual Pear Soufflés (page 180), the Flourless Chocolate Fruit Cake (page 125), or fresh fruit.

Crème Anglaise

1 cup skim milk	3 tablespoons sugar
1/2 cup nonfat liquid egg substitute	1 teaspoon vanilla extract

Warm the milk in a small saucepan over low heat just until it begins to give off steam. Remove from the heat.

Combine the egg substitute and sugar in a mixing bowl, whisking to combine thoroughly. While continuing to whisk, slowly pour in the warm milk. Return the mixture to the saucepan over low heat. Cook for 3 to 4 minutes, stirring constantly, until barely thickened, just enough to lightly coat the back of a spoon.

Pour into a bowl. Stir in the vanilla and serve immediately.

YIELD—ABOUT 1 1/2 CUPS

Fat per tablespoon—0.02 g.
Calories per tablespoon—12.3

Butterscotch Sauce

1/3 cup evaporated skim milk

1/2 tablespoon all-purpose flour

1/2 cup light brown sugar (not packed)

1/4 cup plus 2 tablespoons light corn syrup

Combine the evaporated skim milk and flour in a small bowl, mixing until the flour is thoroughly dissolved.

Put the brown sugar and corn syrup in a small saucepan. Bring to a boil over medium-low heat. Boil for about 4 minutes, stirring occasionally, until a thick syrup forms.

Remove from the heat and cool for 3 minutes. Stir in the evaporated milk mixture. Serve immediately or keep for up to a week in the refrigerator.

YIELD—ABOUT 1 CUP

Fat per tablespoon—0.01 g.

Calories per tablespoon—53.1

Try it on Toffee Crunch Frozen Yogurt (page 168), or on your favorite vanilla frozen yogurt.

Susan's Hot Fudge Sauce

½ tablespoon vanilla extract

½ teaspoon baking powder

¼ cup plus 2 tablespoons unsweetened
   Dutch-processed cocoa powder

2 tablespoons light corn syrup

⅔ cup sugar

3 tablespoons skim milk

Combine the vanilla and baking powder in a small bowl. Mix until smooth and set aside.

In a small, heavy-bottomed saucepan, combine the remaining ingredients. Cook over low heat for about 5 minutes, stirring constantly, until the mixture is thick, smooth, and glossy.

Remove the pan from the heat, add the vanilla mixture, and stir until well incorporated.

The sauce can be used immediately and will thicken quickly as it cools while being served.

YIELD—ABOUT 1 CUP

Fat per tablespoon—0.22 g.
Calories per tablespoon—47.8

Our always supportive literary agent, Susan Ramer, is devoted to both healthy eating and hot fudge sauce, which can be somewhat vexing when it comes time for dessert. We think we've solved her dilemma.

The sauce will keep for up to 3 weeks in the refrigerator and can be reheated.

Strawberry Sauce

¹/₂ pint strawberries, washed, hulled,
  and sliced

2¹/₂ tablespoons freshly squeezed
  orange juice

1 tablespoon sugar

Combine the ingredients in the bowl of a food processor or blender.
Puree until smooth and serve. The sauce may be kept in the refrigerator
for 2 days.

YIELD—ABOUT 1¹/₄ CUPS

Fat per tablespoon—0.05 g.
Calories per tablespoon—6.4

This sauce is so
versatile you just never
seem to have enough
on hand. We use it on
Peaches Poached in
Champagne (page
143), Cappuccino
Angel Food Cake
(page 114), Banana-
Rum Granita (page
166), and Poppy Seed
Cake (page 122), with
or without the Lemon
Glaze. It's also fabulous
on the Russian Cream
(page 178).

In addition to the Cocoa Decadence (page 110) for which it was created, this versatile sauce pairs well with Pear-Port Sorbet (page 164), Chocolate Sorbet (page 162), and Raspberry Mousse (page 177). Try it on the Peaches Poached in Champagne (page 143) instead of the Strawberry Sauce, or on any variety of sliced melon.

Raspberry Sauce

1 cup whole raspberries (plus additional for garnish, optional)

$^1/_2$ tablespoon confectioners' sugar

$^1/_2$ tablespoon freshly squeezed lemon juice

Place the raspberries in a food processor or blender and puree with the confectioners' sugar and lemon juice. Push the puree through a fine mesh strainer to remove the seeds. Cover and chill before serving. The sauce may be kept in the refrigerator for 3 days.

YIELD—ABOUT 1 CUP

Fat per tablespoon—0.04 g.

Calories per tablespoon—5.0

Creamy Yogurt Cheese Frosting

1/3 cup unsweetened frozen apple juice
    concentrate, thawed

1 packet unflavored gelatin

1 cup plain nonfat Yogurt Cheese
    (see Pantry)

2 teaspoons vanilla extract

Put 2 tablespoons of the apple juice concentrate and the gelatin in a small saucepan. Let stand for 2 minutes, then bring to a boil over high heat, stirring to make sure all the gelatin has dissolved. Remove from the heat.

In a large bowl, combine the yogurt cheese, vanilla, and the remaining apple juice concentrate with an electric mixer set at low speed. Beat in the gelatin mixture at medium speed.

Cover and refrigerate for 30 to 45 minutes, until thick and spreadable.

YIELD—ABOUT 1 CUP

Fat per tablespoon—0.02 g.
Calories per tablespoon—14.2

No cream cheese in this creamy frosting—nor sugar—but you'd never know when you taste it on Carrot Cake (page 124). For variety, try it on the Banana Bread Cake (page 109) in place of the Marshmallow Meringue Frosting.

Chocolate Frosting

Rich and old-fashioned tasting— the perfect way to finish our Old-Fashioned Chocolate Cake (page 120), which the kids will love made as cupcakes and topped with this frosting.

1 tablespoon light corn syrup

3 tablespoons unsweetened Dutch-processed cocoa powder

1½ cups confectioners' sugar

¼ cup boiling water

Combine the corn syrup, cocoa powder, confectioners' sugar, and 1 table-spoon of the boiling water in a bowl. Using an electric mixer set at low speed, beat in the rest of the boiling water, a tablespoon at a time, until the mixture is fluffy and glossy.

YIELD—ABOUT 1½ CUPS

Fat per tablespoon—0.07 g.
Calories per tablespoon—33.5

Maple Frosting

2 large eggs, whites only

1/2 cup pure maple syrup

1 tablespoon water

1/4 teaspoon salt

1/2 cup confectioners' sugar

Combine the egg whites, maple syrup, water, and salt in the top of a double boiler over simmering water. (Make sure that the water in the lower pan does not boil up and touch the bottom of the insert.) Cook for about 5 minutes over medium-low heat, whisking constantly until the mixture reaches a temperature of 140 degrees on an instant-read thermometer.

Remove the double boiler from the heat and place the top on a hot pad or towel on a work surface. Using an electric mixer set at medium speed, beat for about 10 minutes, until the beaters begin to trail ribbons over the surface. Add the confectioners' sugar and beat at high speed until thick, spreadable soft peaks begin to form, about 5 minutes.

YIELD—ABOUT 1 1/3 CUPS

Fat per tablespoon—0 g.
Calories per tablespoon—31.5

For an unusually rich taste treat, ice our Old-Fashioned Chocolate Cake (page 120) with this instead of the Chocolate Frosting.

Use this rich and sweet icing on the Banana Bread Cake (page 109) or on the Old-Fashioned Chocolate Cake (page 120), in lieu of Chocolate Frosting.

Marshmallow Meringue Frosting

2 large eggs, whites only

1/4 cup water

2 tablespoons light corn syrup

1/2 cup plus 2 tablespoons granulated sugar

1/4 cup plus 2 tablespoons light brown sugar, firmly packed

Beat the egg whites to stiff peaks with an electric mixer set at medium speed. Set aside.

Combine the water, corn syrup, and sugars in a small saucepan and bring to a boil over medium heat. Boil for about 1 minute, stirring constantly, until the sugar has dissolved.

Beat the syrup into the egg whites at medium speed, continuing to beat until stiff peaks are again formed, about 5 minutes.

YIELD—ABOUT 1 1/3 CUPS

Fat per tablespoon—0 g.
Calories per tablespoon—44.9

Lemon Glaze

2 tablespoons freshly squeezed
   lemon juice

1 cup confectioners' sugar

Whisk the lemon juice and confectioners' sugar in a small bowl. Set aside for 5 minutes before using.

YIELD—ABOUT 1 CUP

Fat per tablespoon—0 g.

Calories per tablespoon—29.4

This tangy glaze works as well on any plain pound cake or angel food cake as it does on our Poppy Seed Cake (page 122).

Index

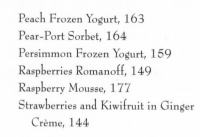